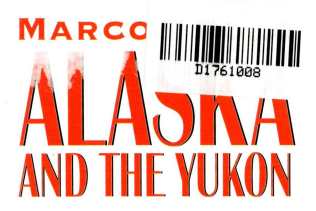

MARCO

ALASKA
AND THE YUKON

with Local Tips

*The author's special recommendations are
highlighted in yellow throughout this guide*

There are five symbols to help you find your way around this guide:

Marco Polo's top recommendations – the best in each category

sites with a scenic view

places where the local people meet

places where young people get together

(100/A1)
*pages and coordinates for the Road Atlas of Alaska and the Yukon
(O) area not covered by maps*

MARCO 🌐 POLO

North America:
Marco Polo North America
70 Bloor Street East
Oshawa, Ontario, Canada
(B) 905-436-2525

United Kingdom:
GeoCenter International Ltd
The Viables Centre
Harrow Way
Basingstoke, Hants RG22 4BJ

Cover photograph: Image Bank: Grant Faint
Photos: author (8, 12, 18, 21, 28, 36, 54, 56, 64, 70, 72, 75, 81, 85);
R. E. Jung (4, 6, 14, 22, 24, 34, 38, 44, 47, 48, 52); Lade: BAV (59); Mauritius: Hubatka (99),
Madersbacher (78); Schapowalow: Dietrich (63); Schuster: Bernhart (66), Liaison (16), Meyers (41)

1ˢᵗ edition 2000
© Mairs Geographischer Verlag, Ostfildern, Germany
Author: Karl Teuschl
Translator: Joan Clough
English edition 2000: Gaia Text
Editorial director: Ferdinand Ranft
Chief editor: Marion Zorn
Cartography for the Road Atlas: © Verlag Haupka & Co., Bad Soden;
Mairs Geographischer Verlag, Ostfildern
Design and layout: Thienhaus/Wippermann
Printed in Germany

CONTENTS

Introduction: Discover Alaska! **5**
Quiet fjords, lonely tundra, rugged mountains –
Alaska is one of the world's last wildernesses

History at a glance **11**

Alaska in context: Bears and wilderness lodges **13**
Bush pilots are Alaska's cab-drivers –
things you ought to know about Alaska

Food & drink: Muktuk and reindeer steaks **19**
American food is served in coffee shops, but Alaska
has regional specialities, too

Shopping & souvenirs: Ulus and Mukluks **23**
Souvenirs are expensive in the far North, but some are really
worth the price

Events: Pioneer festivals and dog-sled races **25**
Alaskans love to celebrate outdoors, in summer and in winter –
even in sub-zero weather

Anchorage: A wilderness metropolis **29**
As the gateway to Alaska, Anchorage is where most trips begin
and where to stock up on supplies

South Alaska/The Kenai Peninsula: Scenic Alaska **37**
The South is the most developed region –
and the most beautiful

Central Alaska/Fairbanks: The highest peak and the biggest river . . . **49**
The country between the Yukon River and the white peaks
of the Alaska Range is vast

Southeast Alaska/The Panhandle: Land of fjords and forests **57**
Explore Southeast Alaska's labyrinth
of islands by ship

The Alaskan bush: Where all roads end **73**
Wild country, lonely tundra and gale-battered islands –
trips that call for careful planning

The Yukon/The Alaska Highway: In Jack London's footsteps **79**
The call of the wild will lure you like the gold prospectors of yore
to the Yukon Territory

Routes in Alaska and the Yukon **87**

Essentials: Practical information **91**

Do's and don'ts **98**

Road Atlas of Alaska and the Yukon **99**

Index **111**

What do you get for your money? **112**

Discover Alaska!

Quiet fjords, lonely tundra, rugged mountains –
Alaska is one of the world's last wildernesses

A*lyeska*, 'great country', is what the Alaskan mainland was called by the native Aleuts, whose wind-tossed chain of tiny islands is scattered across the northern Pacific like a chain of beads. The earliest Russian explorers and fur traders reached Alaska from Siberia. They named the territory after the Aleuts and went home to tell fabulous tales of the mysterious wild country where the sea otter pelts were so handsome that they were worth their weight in gold in China. A myth was born – the dream of a distant, huge and untouched country with untold natural resources just waiting to be discovered.

This dream is alive today. The call of the northern wilds is still enticing, perhaps even more so than in the past since wilderness has become so rare. What you first notice on a trip through Alaska is the sheer size of the country. Of course fjords and glaciers are a familiar sight from pictures of Norway, Sweden and Finland. However, everything's

The lonely expanses
of Denali National Park

bigger in Alaska. Finland boasts a million lakes, but Alaska has three million of them – not to mention 3,000 rivers and a coastline stretching for 80,000 kilometres.

Alaska covers an area of 1.7 million km^2. It is far larger than all the Scandinavian countries together. Yet the population of the 49th US state is only about 620,000, distributed across an area 7.4 times as large as Great Britain. Statistically speaking, that leaves 2.7 km^2 for each Alaskan, a fantastically low population density. In Britain, by contrast, there are only 0.004 km^2 per person. Another factor distorts the statistics even more in Alaska. More than half the population lives in Anchorage, Alaska's only big city. Another 80,000 live in and around Fairbanks. That leaves a lot of uninhabited wilderness, much of it still as unspoilt as it was when the first Russian explorers reached it. No wonder that nature reserves, national parks and national forests take up more than half of the state.

To understand the Alaskan myth, one must remember the

5

role played by the vastness of the territory and the climate, which is harsh and forbidding despite Alaska's wealth of natural resources. The call of the wild lured pioneering adventurers to the far North and Alaska either broke them or made their fortunes, if they were lucky. Alaska abounds in life histories, which have become the stuff of trappers' and gold prospectors' tales. Few pioneers survived long yet this, too, is part of the Alaskan mystique.

The Russians barely scratched the surface of the wilderness. They built a few outposts along the southern coast, hunted otter and spent long, solitary, dark winters in their stockades. A mere century later they sold their colony to the Americans because the Tsar needed money. At first the Americans didn't quite know what to do with their new territory, 'Seward's Folly' as it was called after the Secretary of State who had negotiated the purchase. Gold was discovered in 1900, first on the Klondike, then in Nome and near Fairbanks. Alaska was divulging her secrets and thousands of gold-seekers flocked north.

From then on Alaska was news. Jack London eulogized the wild North and the hard lives led by the gold prospectors in stories based on his own experience, which are still inspiring. Charlie Chaplin made the

Dreams of the fur trading days are conjured up around an Alaska campfire

In the spirit of Marco Polo

Marco Polo was the first true world traveller. He travelled with peaceful intentions forging links between the East and the West. His aim was to discover the world, and explore different cultures and environments without changing or disrupting them. He is an excellent role model for the travellers of today and the future. Wherever we travel we should show respect for other peoples and the natural world.

poignant film *Gold Rush*, in which the character he portrayed was so down and out that he had to carve up his shoe and eat it. Johnny Horton sang 'North to Alaska' – fuel for the Alaska myth.

Black gold was discovered on the North Slope in the 1950s and big, new camps sprang up along the Arctic Sea during the 1970s. It was the Gold Rush all over again. Now the far North was flaunting a new treasure, in this case oil and Alaska boomed again. Americans have come to view Alaska as the last frontier, the last spot on earth for pioneers and adventurers, the only place on the continent not yet touched for better or for worse by civilization.

Lofty expectations you might think, but Alaska more than meets them. The northernmost state of the Union has always fascinated visitors with its unique fauna and astonishing geographical diversity. Fringed with fretwork islands, Southeast Alaska is covered with dense temperate rain forests of Sitka spruce 180 feet high. The Panhandle, a narrow strip of islands and fjords which extends south along the Pacific for 800 km like the 'handle' of a pan, is the spectacular habitat of

whales and bald eagles, the American emblem. Tlingit totem poles guard old fishing villages and salmon swim up the rivers to spawn, not yet threatened by environmental pollution. The Inside Passage, the legendary sea route threading the flotsam of islands taken by the prospectors in the Gold Rush, is still the only reliable link between the region's towns.

If you continue north, you will reach South Alaska. The region around Anchorage and the Kenai Peninsula is the most populous and developed region of Alaska, but that's not saying much. Panoramas of glaciers await you in Prince William Sound, in Kenai Fjords National Park and in the Chugach Mountains, all so much more sublime than nature films on television have led you to believe. Moose graze in the river valleys, seals bask in the sun on drift ice in the fjords and myriad waterfowl hover, suspended above sombre cliffs.

This is the place to jettison a cliché. It simply isn't true that Alaska is buried under snow and ice all year round. The only glaciers the state has are in the mountains of South and Southeast Alaska and the Alaska

Comfort in the wilderness: a B & B inn at Talkeetna

Range, the central massif that bisects the country. But Alaska's glaciers are grandiose. The biggest is the Bering Glacier, which flows majestically and inexorably from the Bagley Ice Field in the Chugach Mountains for 160 km to the Gulf of Alaska. Continue north with your finger on the map. The Alaska Range, with Mt. McKinley, at 6,194 m North America's highest peak, abruptly divides southern from central Alaska. If you go to Alaska, you mustn't miss Denali National Park, which surrounds the vast icy peak. This is your best chance of seeing grizzlies and carabou in their natural habitat. North of the park the Yukon Valley stretches as far as the eye can see and the sun will probably be shining. In summer central

Alaska has the state's best weather: days registering 30°C (86°F) are not infrequent. This region was settled at the end of the 19th and the beginning of the present century because gold was discovered near what is now Fairbanks. Settlement brought a railway and roads. Nonetheless the region has never really been civilized. Men are still prospecting for gold on lonely streams in the Fairbanks hinterland. Wolves howl at night in the woods and in winter the thermometer can drop to –40°C (–40°F).

What you come to at last on your trip north is the Alaska back country, the lonely tundra region bordering the Arctic Ocean and the Bering Sea. Here lie the uncharted fastnesses of the Brooks Range and the foggy

Aleutian Islands, often lashed by fierce gales. It's a good thing the scattered Inuit settlements are now linked by airports and television. Although alcohol and reckless driving have taken their toll on Alaska's native inhabitants, the vast country lies pristine under the Midnight Sun. Huge caribou herds pass through the hills of Kobuk Valley National Park. Wild geese and other seabirds nest in the labyrinth of lakes lacing the Yukon Delta. Enormous brown bears assemble to hunt salmon at their spawning grounds in Katmai National Park.

With a few exceptions, you can explore only on expeditions, which must be planned long in advance. To go on an expedition, you have to be fit. It's advisable to hire a guide for your first venture into the wilderness. He'll know the region and how to survive in it if necessary.

However, for all its savage grandeur and isolation from the rest of the word, Alaska has an amazingly well developed tourist infrastructure. You can explore Alaska comfortably by cruise ship, by hired car at your leisure or even by caravan. If you feel up to it, you can pack a rucksack and tent. There are paved roads for a rewarding round trip: from Anchorage via Fairbanks, Delta Junction and Valdez and back to Anchorage. If you have enough time, you can drive the legendary, 2,300-km-long Alaska Highway from south to north. It is lined with good motels, Bed & Breakfast inns and magnificently situated camping sites. Trails, boat trips and sightseeing flights will also take you into the back country. And don't neglect the side-roads. They'll take you on many a nostalgic trip through such back country towns as Talkeetna, Circle or Eagle.

The second region explored in this guide is also exciting, with lots of pioneer spirit and scenery that is just as grand: the Yukon Territory (popularly known simply as the Yukon), which borders Alaska to the east. This is the country that became at least as famous as Alaska itself in Gold-Rush days on the Klondike. Covering 500,000 km^2, politically, the region belongs to Canada and is administered from Ottawa. Nevertheless, historically and physically, it is inextricably bound up with its bigger neighbour, Alaska. It looks and feels like Alaska and its modern tourist infrastructure is entirely linked up with it. Therefore, it makes good sense to cross the border into the Yukon.

You-con, 'great water', is what the Indians called the mighty river that flows across the North into the Bering Sea. Later the entire region on the upper reaches of the river was named after it. In prehistoric times the broad Yukon Valley saw vast migrations of peoples from across the Bering Strait. It was the corridor through which the ancestors of the modern Native Americans crossed Alaska on their way south to settle the Americas over the course of thousands of years.

During the past century people have been migrating in the opposite direction. The Yukon was the starting point for the European settlers of Alaska. In 1898 the Gold Rush marked the start of the conquest of the north. Adventurous prospectors moved on to the gold-fields around Fairbanks and Nome. Finally, during World War II, the Alaska Highway was built to cut straight across the Yukon, which facilitated the forward thrust of modern civilization into the northwestern corner of the state of Alaska.

The scenery looks much the same on both sides of the border between Alaska and Canada. The broad plains of the Yukon Valley sweep from central Alaska up to the northern spurs of the Rocky Mountains, which bisect the state from north to south. The highest peaks of this mountain chain are in the southern Yukon in the St. Elias Mountains, where the trackless wilderness of Kluane National Park boasts icy summits soaring to nearly 6,000 m. This mighty mountain barrier protects the Yukon from the clouds that build up in the Gulf of Alaska to the west. Consequently, summers in the Yukon are generally hot and sunny. Winters there, however, are bitterly cold. In February 1947 Canada's coldest night on record was registered in the north at Old Crow: –63°C (–81°F).

Certainly summer is the time to go to the Yukon, when the days are warm and the Yukon can flaunt its beauty. The old gold-fields along the Klondike River are still caught up in the pioneer spirit of the Gold Rush days. Dawson City, once styled the 'Paris of the North', does everything to keep memories of the boom era alive. A visit to the Klondike is simply a must if you're going north. From there you can venture out into the vast, unexplored country. You can take a panoramic drive along the Top of the World Highway or leave for a tour along the Dempster Highway into the Mackenzie River delta. Or you might prefer to paddle along the gently flowing Yukon River or take a rafting excursion down the Alsek or the Tatshenshini rivers. Cutting through rocky gorges on their way through the coast range, they both offer superb white-water rafting opportunities. There's something special awaiting hikers. You can follow the historic trail taken years before by the gold prospectors from Skagway through the Chilkoot Pass. Backpacking through the coastal range, you'll get the authentic feel of the rugged pioneer days in the Yukon.

Don't spend too much time touring the far North. A round trip with plenty of time for backpacking and perhaps a flight into the back country with an experienced local bush pilot or a stay at a wilderness lodge is probably enough to keep you busy on a three-week holiday. A trip on the state ferry up through the islands and mountains of the Inside Passage, a stay at a fishing lodge or a trip by rubber dinghy down a remote river and you've already extended your holiday into a fourth week. Alaska is the place for adventure holidays. Though it might take a while for you to feel at home, eventually, either while sitting around the campfire or enjoying the view across a majestic fjord or of Mt. McKinley, you'll realize that you too have succumbed entirely to the magic of Alaska.

History at a glance

From 28,000 BC
Palao Indians migrate across the Bering Strait from Siberia to Alaska

AD 1741
Vitus Bering discovers Alaska and lands on Kayak Island. Reports of valuable sea-otter pelts lead to the Russian colonization of Alaska

1799
Alexander Baranof, first governor of Russian America, founds Sitka and makes it the capital of his furtrading empire

18 October 1867
Russia sells its colony to the US for 7.2 million dollars

1896
Gold on the Klondike! In 1898 near Nome and in 1902 in the Fairbanks region

1912
Alaska becomes a self-governing territory

1917
The wilderness around Mt. McKinley becomes Alaska's first national park

1935
The US government settles southern farmers in the Matanuska Valley, which grows into a productive agricultural region

1942
Construction of the Alaska Highway, still the only land route to Alaska. Military bases are built throughout Alaska. Hundreds of planes fly Lend-Lease supplies from them to Russia

1957
The Alaska oil boom begins

3 January 1959
Alaska becomes the 49th US state

27 March 1964
At 5.36 pm South Alaska is hit by the most severe earthquake ever recorded in North America

1968
Oil is discovered on the Northern Slope at Prudhoe Bay on the Beaufort Sea

1971
The Alaska Native Claims Settlement Act recognizes the rights of native Alaskans. Indians and Eskimos receive 18 million ha of land and 900 million dollars, invested in 13 newly founded Native Corporations

1974–77
The Alyeska Pipeline is built from Prudhoe Bay to Valdez

1989
Twenty-five years after the great earthquake disaster strikes again: the oil tanker *Exxon Valdez* runs aground and 42 million l of oil flow into the Gulf of Alaska

1992
First contact in 50 years between Alaska and Siberia

1999
The Canadian Inuit are granted their own territory: Nunavut

Bears and wilderness lodges

*Bush pilots are Alaska's cab-drivers –
things you ought to know about Alaska*

Bears

You're hardly likely to run into polar bears during your Alaska trip. The white giants inhabit the pack-ice zone bordering the coast of the Beaufort Sea and the Bering Strait. Still you might make the acquaintance of the polar bear's smaller cousin, the black bear, say, weighing up to 90 kg. They are native to the south and to the Panhandle. The title of King of the Wilderness goes to the grizzly. Grizzlies are everywhere except for a few islands. In the interior of Alaska they feed on roots, berries and small animals, growing to an impressive 200–300 kg. Along the coast and on Kodiak Island, where they can eat their fill of fat, tasty salmon, the shaggy giants, called brown bears here, have been known to tip the scales at 600 kg. When the salmon come up the rivers to spawn, dozens of these mammoth bears assemble, waiting to snap them up. However, if you want to watch brown bears feeding on salmon on the McNeil River, Pack Creek and in Katmai National Park or on Kodiak Island, you'll have to plan well in advance. The Alaska State Division of Tourism will send you an information sheet with all you need to know about signing up for a trip.

Needless to say, you must be careful at all times in bear country. Don't take any food (especially sweets) into your tent and see to it that you make noise while hiking. A surprised bear can turn nasty!

Bush pilots

Alaska's road network is about 22,000 km long. Most of the state can be travelled only by air taxis piloted by experienced local pilots. Small towns, lakes and nature reserves in the back country can be reached only by float plane. About 10,000 planes are registered in Alaska. That amounts to one for every 60 inhabitants. There are more than 500 authorized airports, not counting wilderness lakes and gravel banks. Since the first plane flew out to McGrath pros-

*Traditions kept alive:
an Indian at the Tlingit festival
in Juneau*

Amphibious planes – often the only transport available into the wilds

pecting camp from Fairbanks in 1924, bush pilots have been inextricably intertwined with Alaska's pioneer history. The daring exploits of pilots like Ben Eielson and Don Sheldon are the stuff of legend. Not all the emergency landings and rescue operations undertaken in this wild country have been successful. Such flights are still hazardous. Before take-off, you're advised to take a good look at the emergency equipment and radio transmitter, which safety regulations require every plane to carry.

Earthquakes and volcanoes

Alaska forms part of a tectonically unstable region known as the 'ring of fire', which is constantly shaken by headline-grabbing earthquakes and volcanic eruptions. The cause is continental drift. Far beneath the southern coast of Alaska and the Aleutian Islands, the Pacific plate is sliding under the North American plate, producing a ceaseless series of fissures and cracks. About 40 volcanoes have erupted in Alaska since records have been kept. The most severe eruption took place in 1912 in what is now Katmai National Park. In recent years, too, volcanic eruptions have been recorded, among them Mt. Augustine on Cook Inlet in 1986 and in 1992 Mt. Spurr west of Anchorage. The same holds for earthquakes. The 1964 Good Friday quake registered 8.6 on the Richter scale, the most severe earthquake ever recorded in North America. It caused a great deal of damage to southern Alaska ports. Nevertheless, Alaska earthquakes are usually harmless since most occur in the uninhabited parts of the Aleutian Islands.

The Inuit and Native Americans

At least 100,000 of Alaska's total population of 620,000 are descendants of the Great Country's former overlords. The Tlingit, Haida and Tsimshian Indians live in the south. The Dena tribes inhabit the interior and the Canadian Yukon territory. The Inuit, called Eskimos in popular parlance, inhabit the bleak coasts of the Beaufort Sea and the Bering Strait. In addition, a third, often overlooked, ethnic group still lives on the Pribilof Islands and in some small settlements on the stormy and fog-bound Aleutian Islands.

Most Alaskans of European descent live in the south while Native Americans still inhabit the vast interior. The 1971 Alaska Native Claims Settlement Act allocated money and millions of acres of land to 13 corporations representing Alaska's native peoples. Most of these native Alaskan corporations make profits but life is rugged for the people living in the scattered settlements. Alcohol and boredom cause the worst problems. Once hunters and gatherers, the native peoples of Alaska are alienated from their age-old way of life, and the modern American lifestyle cannot replace it.

Gold

Gold has played a bigger role in Alaska's history than all other natural resources combined. It has lured more people to the north and has remained the stuff of dream and legend to this day. As early as 1848 the Russians discovered gold on the Kenai Peninsula. The first real strike came in 1880 in Juneau and soon afterwards gold was found in the Forty Mile Region. Then the discovery of the vast Klondike goldfields in the Yukon in 1896 ushered in the biggest Gold Rush of all time.

More than 100,000 gold-seekers trekked through the notorious Chilkoot Pass on their way to the Klondike. Three boom years saw a gold harvest worth 100 million dollars, followed by strikes at Nome in 1889 and Fairbanks in 1902. Prospectors are still panning the Alaskan rivers for gold in the Fairbanks region. In 1996 approximately 180,000 ounces of gold worth about 60 million dollars were brought to light in Alaska.

Salmon

Every fly-fisherman dreams of going to Alaska for the salmon fishing. This understandable wish poses no problem at all since Alaska abounds in salmon of all kinds. In a good year 40 million sockeye salmon come to Bristol Bay alone to spawn. Alaska boasts five different species of this fish prized by sportsmen and gourmets alike: small chum and pink salmon, sockeye salmon, which is also known as the red salmon, silver salmon and, biggest and most famous of all, the king salmon. A king salmon can weigh in at more than 40 kg. After several years spent in the salt waters of the open ocean, all Pacific salmon return to their native rivers to spawn. As if following inner radar impulses, they buck the current in the thousands, leaping all obstacles to reach the very streams where they were born. There they spawn and die. Each fish seems to recognize the stream it originally came from by its taste. Visitors to Alaska can observe the awe-inspiring natural spectacle of salmon runs every summer along easily accessible Southeast Alaskan streams and on the Kenai Peninsula.

The oil pipeline

Alaska's biggest building project runs for nearly 1,300 km. The gleaming Alyeska Pipeline, as it is officially called, bisects Alaska from Prudhoe Bay on the Beaufort Sea in the north to the southern port of Valdez on the Gulf of Alaska, called at by oil tankers. For nearly half its length the Trans-Alaska Pipeline is elevated above the ground on 78,000 piles to keep it from thawing the permafrost. Building the pipeline took two years and cost nine billion dollars. Oil started flowing through it on 20 June 1977. To date it has transported more than ten billion barrels of crude oil, bringing prosperity but also disaster. In March 1989 the Tanker *Exxon Valdez* struck Bligh Reef in Prince William Sound. South Alaska was polluted as far as Kodiak Island by 42 million litres of crude oil.

Permafrost

Permafrost is created anywhere the annual mean temperature remains below 0 °C. This is the case in much of Alaska. On the North Slope, north of the transverse Brooks Range, the groundwater remains frozen for years on end. Even at mid-summer only the upper layer of soil thaws out. This is one major factor that makes hiking or building houses such difficult propositions in the North. Meltwater on top of frozen soil turns building sites into a thick mire. Some tough tundra plants often grow from a layer of soil only a few centimetres thick covering the dense ice from ancient lakes. During the last glaciation per-

Wearing furs makes sense

iods, central Alaska and the Yukon were not covered by protecting glaciers so that the cold was free to seep into the ground for millennia and keep it frozen solid. Consequently, in some regions of Alaska, the permafrost layer is well over 1,000 m thick.

Politics

For over a century Alaska was a Russian colony. Purchased from Russia in 1867, it spent another century as an independent territory administered by the United States before becoming the 49th state in 1959 with Juneau as its capital. The state government is typical of the US political system as a whole: the bicameral state legislature consists of a Senate with 25 members and a House of Representatives with 40. The state is governed by a governor and his cabinet. Gubernatorial elections are held every four years. Alaska has two senators in Washington and, because it has such a small overall population, it sends only one member to the House of Representatives.

Natural resources and the economy

There has never been any manufacturing in Alaska. Since it was colonized by the Russians in the mid-18th century, Alaska's economy has consisted of the often reckless exploitation of its natural resources. It is so rich in them and so vast that they have, fortunately, not been seriously depleted. Fur and gold were the first natural resources to be exploited. Now oil takes pride of place and brings in by far the most revenue. Alaska has such enormous oil reserves that the state has no need for a state income tax. In fact it sends every US citizen registered as an Alaska resident an annual cheque as his or her dividends from oil revenue. The tundra of the North Slope still conceals at least six billion barrels of crude oil. Other lucrative sources of income in Alaska include tourism, logging (especially in Southeast Alaska) and fishing as well as fish hatcheries (in the Gulf of Alaska and the Bering Sea).

Totem poles

The Native American tribes in the Panhandle are the Tlingit and the Haida. They are Alaska's carving adepts. Nature's bounty in their indigenous regions has granted them leisure to devote themselves to their craft. From the soft wood of the British Columbia red cedar, a species of thuja, they have always carved lavishly decorated masks, chests and canoes. However, the most spectacular symbols of Northwestern culture are totem poles. Stained in bright colours with plant dye, totem poles are like coats of arms, indicating a clan's prestige. Relating myths, they chronicle clan history. Setting up a totem pole was the occasion for a *potlatch*, a big feast with dancing and eating lasting for days.

The heyday of Native American carving set in about 1840 after tools for metalworking became available to the area. European missionaries regarded totem poles as symbols of idolatry and forbade them. Only recently has this ancient art been revived. Nowadays there are workshops and carving schools in Ketchikan, Sitka and Haines, attesting to a renaissance of Native American art and new pride in indigenous culture.

Wilderness lodges

One of the best ways of enjoying Alaska's beautiful scenery is to stay at a wilderness lodge. Scattered throughout the state, these inns provide comfortable accommodation for 10 to 20 guests. Most wilderness lodges are romantic log cabins situated on fjords or back-country lakes, which can be reached only by floatplane. Their appointments can be anything from rustic to luxurious and prices range from $50 to $300 a day. Kayaking, fishing, watching animals and hiking in the wilds are activities offered at most lodges. The food served at them is usually good, hearty fare: salmon, crab, steaks and even moose or elk stew. Although in the wilds, many lodges are famous for their food. In any case you'll have to book stays well in advance, just as you do guided treks into the wilderness. The best lodges are booked up at least six months in advance at peak season so don't wait till the last minute.

Muktuk and reindeer steaks

American food is served in coffee shops,
but Alaska has regional specialities, too

Gourmet cuisine is not the order of the day in Alaska despite the availability of superb salmon. Most eateries serve hearty American food and helpings are generous to say the least. The little roadhouse restaurants along the highways or lodge restaurants have excellent steaks on the menu, any way you like them. Casserole cooking is another old stand-by: perfect for famished hikers just in from the trail!

Don't miss all that superb seafood: fresh salmon and halibut from Alaskan waters are on the menu nearly everywhere. Be sure you give fish breaded in stale batter and fried a wide berth; you want yours *grilled, sauteed* (quickly pan-fried) or *broiled* (in the oven). King and silver salmon are generally regarded as the best varieties of this noble fish. Silver salmon is especially good from the Copper River. Its icy waters are fed by melting glaciers so the fish develop a fine marbling of fat to protect themselves against the cold. Mussels and crab are usually on the menu near the coast. You'll love the chewy, tasty sourdough bread served with your meals there.

Although the sea has been so bounteous to Alaskan cuisine, agricultural produce isn't so readily available. You'll find roadhouses famous for their blueberry pancakes. A wilderness lodge might serve bunchberry marmelade made of red berries from the tundra. Another wild delicacy is steamed fiddle-head ferns as a side-dish or salad.

Restaurant prices are in the high range since everything you eat, especially in the back country, has to be transported a long, arduous way or even flown in. If you choose the self-catering option on a camping trip, you'll have to buy all the provisions you need in the well-stocked Anchorage supermarkets before setting out. Little general stores in the back country usually don't stock much more than frozen mince for hamburgers and canned vegetables. The freeze-dried food of the type available in all Alaskan sporting goods stores makes the best provisions for long hiking trips.

Fresh from the Bering Sea:
Alaskan king crab

But aren't there any real Alaskan specialities? Well, in the whale-hunting season (the Inuit are permitted to hunt whales) you might give muktuk a try if you're anywhere near the Barrow Inuit and feel really venturesome. This is whale blubber, cut up into tiny pieces and eaten raw. If muktuk is not to your liking, you're sure to enjoy the world-famous giant Alaska king crabs from the icy deeps of the Bering Strait. They are usually on the menu in better restaurants.

You might expect to find game on the menu in Alaska: tender wild duck or juicy caribou steaks. You'll be disappointed. Although Alaska boasts game in plenty, it may not be sold for human consumption without an official permit. Only very few restaurants have one. Alaskans and Canadians hunt for their own tables so you'll probably be served game only if you happen to be invited to a meal by an Alaskan family. The hunting season is in autumn so, by the time visitors arrive the following spring, all the delicious frozen caribou and elk steaks have long since been eaten up.

Reindeer steaks or sausages are quite often on the menu because the Inuit of Nome have been breeding reindeer since the late 19th century, when they were introduced to Alaska from Lapland. Some butchers in and around Anchorage sell beef jerky or even pemmican, meat from game animals, ground, spiced and slowly dried: great snacks for camping and hiking! If you want to live off the land, you can enjoy succulent trout from lakes and raging streams or juicy huckleberries and, only if you know what you're doing, wild mushrooms.

Restaurants

For breakfast you'll go to a coffee shop. Most hotels and lodges have one. What you'll find to eat there, though, is invariably the hearty American breakfast that will stick to your ribs all day. It includes eggs *(sunny side up =* fried on one side only, overeasy = turned over, or *scrambled)*, sausages *(even game sausages)*, bacon (Canadian, which is like British rashers, or American) or ham as well as fried potatoes *(hash browns)* and toast with marmelade. You should really try *French toast* (bread fritters served with corn or maple syrup or jam), *pancakes* or an omelette. If you're not really all that hungry, you'd be better off ordering a *continental breakfast*: coffee, orange juice and toast or muffins. Your cup of coffee – either full-strength or decaffeinated – will be replenished until you'll have to simply say no.

Americans tend to eat light lunches, served between 12 noon and 2 pm. What is served for lunch is usually listed separately on the restaurant bill of fare *(lunch menu)* for instance *soup and salad*, sandwiches with all sorts of fillings served on various types of bread like whole wheat (granary) or rye as well as white and hamburgers.

The evening meal *(dinner)* is served in rural areas as early as 6 or 7 pm; in towns and cities anywhere from 7 to 9 pm. As is usual throughout the United States, you either have to book a table in advance or queue up and wait until a table is free. A waiter or waitress will ask that you wait to be seated. The ambience is totally informal in most wilderness lodges.

In some of them you may even find yourself washing up the serviceable metal tableware. There are, however, quite a few very luxurious lodges, where you dine on fine china by candlelight. Some of these are renowned for excitingly innovative gourmet cuisine.

The prices given on restaurant menus do not include a service charge *(tips)* or even tax, which varies from place to place. The tax, however, will be itemized on your bill. You can leave your tip (about 15 per cent of the bill) on the table or simply hand it to your waiter or waitress. But do remember to tip.

Drinks

Alaska is beer country. Beer is served ice-cold, and what you'll usually find is Budweiser, Schlitz or Coors. Don't despair. There are better beers, brewed in small local breweries, just as there are now throughout the United States. These include Alaskan Amber or the British-style Canadian beers like Molson Canadian or Labatt's Blue. Wine is available in good restaurants. It's usually Californian, ranging from plonk to world-class vintages.

Devotees of strong drink can always find American bourbon, Canadian whisky or Scotch. These whiskies are usually served on ice *(on the rocks)* or, like rum or gin, in the form of cocktails. Yukon Jack, a whisky liqueur that is really firewater, is an Alaskan speciality. This is one way of keeping warm during those long, cold winter nights, but expect hideous hangovers.

In addition to the usual hotel bars you'll find in cities, you'll enjoy the rustic back-woods bars with stuffed mooseheads on the walls and long, Western-style bars. This is often the best place to meet 'sourdoughs' (dyed-in-the-wool Alaskans). A Canadian entertainment import is what is known as a *cabaret*. It's really just a big bar, often with live country & western music.

Back-country hospitality: the Nugget Inn in Nome

Ulus and Mukluks

*Souvenirs are expensive in the far North,
but some are really worth the price*

The shopping malls and super-markets so typical of the United States are found only in Anchorage, Fairbanks and a few other large towns. You'll notice that prices for goods are up to 25 per cent higher than they would be in most other parts of the US because everything has to be flown or shipped in. Fresh farm produce may even be marked up 200 to 300 per cent. You're advised to stock up on staple commodities and supplies in Anchorage before going off on trips.

Souvenirs 'Made in Taiwan' abound in the type of shops you'd expect to carry them. But there are also lots of lovely Alaskan things to take home. What about an ulu, a typical Inuit knife? They're great for dicing vegetables and slicing meat. Then there are Arctic parkas, anoraks with bright-coloured embroidery, and sweaters etc. knitted of qiviut, the wool of the Arctic musk-ox. The Inuit also make heavy fur boots, which you may not find much use for at home but, then again, you never know when they might come in handy. A pair of these mukluks on your wall is not to be sneezed at.

Decorating à la Alaska

Gold-nugget jewellery is sold in the Canadian Yukon Territory and throughout Alaska, particularly in the gold-field regions around Dawson City and Fairbanks. Some regional specialities make good souvenirs for leisurely consumption at home: fireweed honey, smoked salmon or Alaskan wild berry jam. Modern art galleries bait culture vultures with paintings, sculpture and arty jewellery with Alaskan motifs. Of course there's a lot of kitsch but some young artists as well as renowned ones like Rie Munoz and Barbara Lavellee produce good work.

The best souvenirs – unfortunately expensive – are genuine Inuit and Native American arts and crafts. The Dena Indians still make their traditional elk-skin moccasins, baskets decorated with porcupine quills and bead-embroidered jackets. The Tlingit of Southeast Alaska, once renowned for their totem poles, carve smaller objects and transfer their traditional stylized animal symbols to silver jewellery and drawings. Inuit soapstone and nephrite sculpture is world-famous. It is sold at city art galleries, some of them internationally known. Prices start at about $200 but can be much higher.

Pioneer festivals and dog-sled races

Alaskans love to celebrate outdoors, in summer and in winter – even in sub-zero weather

Even though life is rugged in Alaska, or perhaps just because it is, Alaskans live by the motto work hard and play hard. Most Alaskan festivities are loud, tough and decidedly informal affairs. Beer is dispensed by the keg. You're invited to measure your skills and strength with the locals at sawing wood or canoe racing.

Pioneer festivals are lots of fun, especially in small towns. Funny parades, fairs and contests celebrate the short but stirring history of this northernmost state of the Union. If you want to know what's on over the weekend, go to your local Visitors' Centre for the full events calendar.

Most coastal towns and cities host an event for salmon fishers, a *Salmon Derby*. Bird-watchers can observe the spring bird migrations at numerous *Bird Festivals* accompanied by lectures and tours guided by ornithologists. Trappers meet in winter for fur auctions.

Finally, and most famously, there are dog-sled races throughout Alaska, many of them highly lucrative for the winners. After all, *dog sledding* is the official state sport. By contrast, religious holidays don't seem to count for as much in Alaska and the Yukon. In most cities, shops remain open. US national holidays are usually on a Monday to make a long weekend – for Alaskans, as for most hard-working US citizens, a welcome short holiday. The peak summer season is framed by two of these long weekends: Memorial Day at the end of May marks the beginning of summer and it ends at Labor Day Weekend, the first weekend in September, when the school year starts again throughout the US.

PUBLIC HOLIDAYS

Banks, schools, post offices and many museums are closed on the following national holidays:
1st January *New Year's Day*
3rd Monday in January *Martin Luther King Jr. Day*
3rd Monday in February *Presidents' Day*

The trapper's best friend

MARCO POLO SELECTION: EVENTS

1 Iditarod Race
The world's toughest and certainly most famous dog-sled race (page 26)

2 Klondike International Outhouse Race
About as funny as it comes! (page 27)

3 Talkeetna Moose Dropping Festival
Quaint pioneer festival with dancing, fun and contests (page 27)

4 World Eskimo-Indian Olympics
Unheard of sports, such as ear-pulling contests (page 27)

3rd Monday in March *Seward's Day* (celebrating Seward's purchase of Alaska)

Last Monday in May *Memorial Day* (commemorating war heroes)

4th July *Independence Day*

3rd Monday in August *Discovery Day* (in the Canadian Yukon Territory)

1st Monday in September *Labor Day*

18th October *Alaska Day*

11th November *Veterans Day*

3rd Thursday in November *Thanksgiving Day*

EVENTS & FESTIVALS

February

Anchorage invites everyone to the biggest Alaskan winter event, the *Fur Rendezvous,* featuring a winter carnival, fur auctions, dog-sled racing and skiing events as well as ice-sculpture carving competitions.

Yukon Sourdough Rendezvous. Winter gold-prospectors' festival staged in Whitehorse on the occasion of the Yukon Quest, a dog-sled race over a trail 1,500 km long. During February nu-

merous small Alaskan towns, including Nenana, Ketchikan and Valdez, put on their own *dog-sled races* and host winter carnivals.

March

Anchorage: early in the month the world-renowned ★ *Iditarod Trail Dog Sled Race* begins. 1,049 miles and 14 days later exhausted teams of sled dogs and their drivers arrive in Nome on the Bering Strait, marking the occasion for a boisterous welcome celebration.

April

Fairbanks: *Arctic Man Ski & Sno Go Classic,* a wild race with competing motor sleds and ski teams.

May

Cordova Shorebird Festival. Early in the month on the banks of the Copper River. The ultimate venue for ornithologists and migratory birds.

Homer hosts its own bird-watching event, the *Annual Kachemak Bay Shorebird Festival* at the same time.

Kodiak Island: the island puts on a fair and contests to celebrate its *Crab Festival* in honour of its fabulous king crab.

June

At the weekend of the 21st, the Summer Solstice, Nome throws a *Midnight Sun Festival,* Anchorage stages a *Midnight Sun Marathon* and Skagway hosts its traditional *Solstice Picnic.* Dawson City in Canada puts on a big *Party on the Midnight Dome,* the mountain above the town.

July

❂ The national holidays, *Canada Day* (1st July) and *Independence Day* (4th July), are the scene of picnics and parades, fireworks and street festivals throughout the Yukon and Alaska. Border towns like Hyder, Haines and Eagle celebrate both, with at least four days of festivities.

Dawson City: on 1 July *Gold Panning Championship* and a race to the Midnight Dome.

Seward: on 4th July the traditional *Mt. Marathon Race,* a gruelling race to the top of the nearby 920-m-high mountain, which leaves many weary contestants bloody and battered.

Talkeetna: on the second weekend of the month ★ *Moose Dropping Festival,* a pioneer festival with a costume parade and a big fair.

Fairbanks: on the *Golden Days* at mid-month the city celebrates the Gold-Rush era with a big parade, country music and costume festivals. At the same time the best Native American sportsmen- and women meet for the ★ *World Eskimo-Indian Olympics.*

August

Salmon Derby in Seward, Valdez, Cordova and Juneau.

Valdez: *Gold Rush Days.* A colourful pioneer festival early in the month.

Dawson City: *Discovery Days.* On the 17th the city celebrates the first gold strike in the Yukon Territory with costume parades and boat races.

Fairbanks: lumberjacks, farmers and gold prospectors meet at mid-month for the ❂ *Tanana Valley State Fair,* a large agricultural show with lots of country music, a fair and a presentation of awards for the biggest cabbages statewide. At mid-month Haines puts on the *Southeast Alaska State Fair,* followed by Palmer with the *Alaska State Fair.*

September

Dawson City: the first weekend of the month sees the ★ *Klondike International Outhouse Race* with hilariously decorated outdoor toilets pulled through the streets by people dressed up as gold prospectors.

Kenai, Petersburg, Kodiak and Whittier each have a *Salmon Derby* of their own.

Fair time in Alaska

Fairbanks, Haines and Palmer hold their State Fairs in late summer – but they aren't the simple agricultural produce shows you might expect. These fairs offer you the chance to meet Alaskans – doing Native American dances, playing country music, marching in parades and attending veteran car rallies.

A wilderness metropolis

As the gateway to Alaska, Anchorage is where most trips begin and where to stock up on supplies

Alaskans say: 'You can see Alaska from Anchorage'. You see what they mean when you are about to land at the only metropolis (**102/B4**) in the 49th state. What you see is a typical US city covering a vast area with broad streets laid out on a grid plan, sprawling suburbs and a few massive skyscrapers marking the downtown business

Fourth Avenue: these 'historic' buildings are only about 50 years old

section. The population of Anchorage is about 250,000. Nearly half of all Alaskans live here. However, the outskirts of the city mark the fringes of the wilds. In the east the glacier-clad Chugach Mountains soar to over 2,000 m. Two sparkling bays delimit the broad coastal plane where Anchorage lies. In clear weather you can even see the icy peaks of the Alaska Range to the north. It boasts North America's highest peak, majestic Mt. McKinley (6,194 m).

Hotel and restaurant prices

Hotels
Category 1: hotels and lodges over $150
Category 2: good hotels and motels from $70 to $150
Category 3: modest motels less than $70

Prices are for two people in a double room. Single rooms are not much cheaper. Children usually sleep free of charge in their parents' room.

Restaurants
Category 1: over $35
Category 2: $20 to $35
Category 3: less than $20

Prices are for an evening meal with soup or a starter, a main course and dessert.

Important abbreviations

Ave.	Avenue	**Mt.**	Mount
Blvd.	Boulevard	**Rd.**	Road
Hwy.	Highway	**St.**	Street

MARCO POLO SELECTION: ANCHORAGE

1 Anchorage Museum of History and Art
Alaskan history from mammoth hunters to the oil pipeline (page 31)

2 Lake Hood
The bush pilots' airport: perfect for a trip in a floatplane (page 31)

3 Oomingmak Co-op
This is where you can buy authentic Alaskan souvenirs: knitwear made from musk-ox wool (page 33)

4 Portage Glacier
Icebergs and glacier-covered peaks: the Alaska of your dreams (page 35)

Nature in the raw is never far away from Anchorage. With any luck you may even make the acquaintance of Alaskan fauna right in the city. Only a few streets from the city centre, salmon swim up Ship Creek from Cook Inlet to spawn. Bald eagles, the US national emblem, circle above the creek and you might see a moose standing on the lawn of a house in the lush suburbs or a bear might amble across a street. The animals have not yet come to terms with the fact that all this now belongs to people and not to them. No wonder they still feel at home here: Anchorage is not much more than 80 years old. It started as a camp for men building the Alaska Railroad from Seward to Fairbanks in 1915. Within only a few months the northern end of Cook Inlet had ballooned into a settlement with 2,000 men living in tents. From then on Anchorage grew in fits and starts as boom towns in the far North tend to do. During World War II large military bases were established at Anchorage. Later oil was drilled in Cook Inlet and later still on Prudhoe Bay.

Anchorage became the logistical hub of the northernmost US state and the big oil concerns active in the region had their headquarters here.

There are hardly any old buildings in Anchorage. The reason for this lack is not difficult to discover. The terrible 1964 Good Friday earthquake, which registered a record-breaking 8.6 on the Richter scale, destroyed almost the entire city. Since then Anchorage has been rebuilt to look like any other modern US city with office tower blocks and filling stations, shopping malls and fast-food eateries. Not all that prepossessing, surely, but, nevertheless, if you go to Alaska, you cannot avoid Anchorage because it is at the interface of all the major highways, it has the biggest and most reasonably priced supermarkets and sporting-goods stores and it is in any case the best point of departure for the towns and nature reserves in the back country. Bush pilots usually leave from here to fly visitors out to scenic lakes and wilderness lodges.

☞ City Map inside back cover

SIGHTS

The downtown area is small, centred on the two main business thoroughfares, 4th and 5th Ave., so that you can easily explore it on foot. You won't get lost here. The avenues are numbered from north to south and streets are named in letters from east to west. The best place to start your tour of the city is the corner of 4th Ave. and F St. A little log cabin there houses the city Information Centre. Little shopping malls cluster around it. This is the locale of the beautifully renovated 4th Avenue Theatre, lots of souvenir shops and furriers and some attractive public buildings like the post-modern Performing Arts Centre on 5th Ave. If you're tired of walking, the terminal for the People Mover city buses serving all parts of the city is located conveniently at the corner of 6th Ave. and G St.

Alaska Experience Theatre
A 40-minute film on Alaska shown on a gigantic, curved screen. *705 W 6th Ave., daily noon–6 pm, in summer 9 am–9 pm, admission $7*

Lake Hood
★ Sightseeing of a different kind. This lake near the International Airport is the world's largest amphibious airport. During the summer 800 planes take off and land here daily. Incredible amphibious aircraft and all kinds of small planes. Be careful, however: planes have right of way!

The south shore of the lake is fringed with the offices of the pilots and the air taxi companies that take visitors on scenic flights across the Chugach Mountains. The cost is high, ranging from approximately $80 to $250 for flights lasting from one to three hours in a floatplane. *Ketchum Air Service, Tel. 243 55 25, or Alaska Bush Carriers, Tel. 243 31 27*

Resolution Park
From the wooden platform below the Captain Cook Monument you have a superb ☀ view out across the bay, which the English explorer discovered in 1778. Whales (humpbacks) are often spotted here in summer and autumn. *At the western tip of 3rd Ave.*

MUSEUMS

Alaska Aviation Heritage Museum
Old photos and films document the history of aviation in Alaska. About 25 restored bush planes are kept in large hangars on the south shore of Lake Hood. *4721 Aircraft Drive, in summer daily 9 am–6 pm, admission $5.75*

Alaska Native Heritage Center
A museum village documenting the five Alaskan indigenous peoples: the Inuit, Native American tribes and the Aleuts. *8800 Heritage Center Drive, in summer daily 10 am–8 pm, admission $20*

Anchorage Museum of History and Art
★ The big exhibitions on the first floor give a good survey of Alaskan history and that of its indigenous peoples. The migrations across the Bering Strait as well as modern exploration for oil are explained succinctly. The ground floor is reserved for art from, and dealing with, Alaska. Good museum shop. *121 W 7th Ave., in summer daily 9 am–6 pm, in winter Mon closed, admission $5*

Fancy Moose/Regal Alaskan

🕆 Ideal in sunny weather: you sit on the terrace, watch the amphibious planes, drink beer and eat fresh halibut. *In the Regal Alaskan Hotel, 4800 Spenard Rd., Tel. 243 23 00, Category 3*

Gwennie's

❖ Rustic eatery with pioneer ambience and helpings so hearty you'll need help. Breakfasts include reindeer omelettes and big, floppy pancakes. *4333 Spenard Rd., Tel. 243 20 90, Category 2–3*

Humpy's Great Alaskan Ale House

🕆 Beer and the young crowd, light food like fresh local fish, pasta and salads. Very popular for lunch and a great venue in the evening with live band music. *610 W 6th Ave., Tel. 276 23 37, Category 3*

Sacks Café

❖ Popular and stylish with imaginative Asian and Italian cuisine. *625 W 5th Ave., Tel. 276 35 46, Category 1–2*

Simon & Seaforts

Fresh salmon and steaks with a lovely 💐 view out across Cook Inlet. *420 L St., Tel. 274 35 02, Category 2*

SHOPPING

You can browse for souvenirs in the shops along 4th Ave. Your best bet for camping and hiking equipment as well as provisions for the back country is any one of the big shopping centres along Northern Lights Blvd. At the intersection of Northern Lights Blvd. and Spenard Rd. there are several sporting-goods stores with a wide selection of hiking boots, sleeping bags and tents.

Dimond Mall

Huge shopping mall with 120 shops and department-store outlets on the southern fringe of the city. *Old Seward Hwy./Dimond Blvd.*

Gary King

Everything you'll need for fishing, hunting and camping. *202 E Northern Lights Blvd., Tel. 279 74 54*

From Cheechako to sourdough

A person who has just arrived in Alaska is dubbed a *Cheechako*, a greenhorn, who has no idea at all of how to survive in the wilderness. Not until you have spent a few years – and winters – in the Alaskan bush do you merit the accolade of *sourdough*. This nickname, too, which today is used to designate all long-term residents of rural Alaska, especially dates from the pioneer days. Then trappers and gold prospectors always travelled through the back country with balls of sour dough in their packs. Sometimes all they had was bread and pancakes made of sour dough, flour and water. A tiny bit of sour dough could be topped up with flour and – lo and behold – there was enough for a meal. Some of these yeast cultures are said to have survived for years and even generations. Baking with sourdough is an art.

Oomingmak Co-op

★ Looking for presents from the Arctic Circle? Sweaters and scarves knitted of Arctic musk-ox wool. *604 H St., Tel. 272 92 25*

R. E. I. Inc.

Big sporting-goods store for hiking, kayaking and canoeing. *1200 W Northern Lights Blvd., Tel. 272 45 65*

6th Avenue Outfitters

Wilderness equipment from tents to thermo-boots. *520 W 6th Av., Tel. 276 02 33*

ACCOMMODATION

Alpine Inn

Comfortable bed & breakfast overlooking the city on the slopes of the Chugach Mountains. The German proprietress arranges tours throughout the region and picks up guests at the airport. *4 rooms, P. O. Box 22 00 04, Anchorage, AK 99522, Tel. 274 15 96, Fax 274 15 87, Category 2*

Anchorage Hotel

Elegant hotel with historic ambience and a great deal of charm. Prime downtown location. *26 rooms, 330 E St., Tel. 272 45 53, Fax 277 44 83, Category 1*

Chelsea Inn

An unpretentious, clean hotel situated halfway between downtown and the airport. *45 rooms, 3836 Spenard Rd., Tel. 276 50 02, Fax 277 76 42, Category 2*

Days Inn

Homey comfort on downtown southern fringe. *130 rooms, 321 E 5th Ave., Tel. 276 72 26, Fax 278 60 41, Category 1–2*

Hilton Anchorage

Big luxury hotel at centre of town. *591 rooms, 500 W 3rd Ave., Tel. 272 74 11, Fax 265 71 40, Category 1*

Hostelling Int'l. Anchorage

Comfortable youth hostel at centre of town. Info-Exchange for backpackers and information on all Alaska youth hostels. *95 beds, 700 H St., Tel. 276 36 35, Fax 276 77 72, Category 3*

Stay with a Friend/ Alaska Private Lodgings

Reliable agency for bed & breakfast accommodation all over town and in all price ranges. *704 W 2nd Ave., Anchorage, AK 99501, Tel. 258 17 17, Fax 258 66 13*

SPORTS & LEISURE

Alaskan Bicycle Adventures

Guided one-week cycle tours in Alaska and in the Yukon. Hotel accommodation. *2734 Iliamna Ave., Anchorage, AK 99517, Tel. 243 23 29, Fax 243 49 85*

Fishing

Some of Alaska's best salmon rivers are just north of Anchorage: the Susitna and Deshka rivers and Alexander Creek. The air-taxi companies on Lake Hood can arrange for you to be flown to a lodge in this region or simply fly you up for a glorious day's fishing. *You might book at Ketchum Air Service, Tel. 243 55 25, or Rust's Flying Service, Tel. 243 15 95*

NOVA

White-water rafting trips for one day or as long as you want in the surrounding back country: on the Copper or Matanuska rivers.

The Native American Eklutna Village: dwellings for the souls of the dead

Also canoe trips on Prince William Sound. *P.O. Box 1129, Chickaloon, AK 99674, Tel. 745 57 53, Fax 745 57 54*

ENTERTAINMENT

Numerous bars and nightclubs are clustered downtown and especially along Spenard Rd. If you want a taste of the robust pioneer nightlife, the place for you might be the ❖ *Great Alaskan Bush Company (631 E International Airport Rd.)*, where you can drink beer and watch strippers take it all off. For an evening of less macho amusement ♣ *Chilkoot Charlie's (2435 Spenard Rd.)*, a big Gold Rush-style saloon with two dance floors.

INFORMATION

Anchorage Convention & Visitors' Bureau
Infostand at the corner of W 4th Ave./ F St. Postal address: 524 W 4th Ave., Anchorage, AK 99501, Tel. 274 35 31, Fax 278 55 59

Alaska Public Lands Information Center (APLC)
Good information material and individual consulting on all Alaska nature reserves. You can book camping sites and wilderness cabins in the national forests here. *605 W 4th Ave., Anchorage, AK 99501, Tel. 271 27 37, Fax 271 27 44*

SURROUNDING AREA

Alyeska Resort/ Girdwood   (102/B5)
A broad valley in the Chugach Mountains about 60 km southeast of Anchorage (on Hwy. 1), it is Alaska's only completely developed skiing area (and quite a good one, too), replete with an elegant resort and holiday flats. In 1992 the area even applied to be the venue of the Winter Olympics. In summer gondola cars take visitors up the 1,201-m-high peak of *Mt. Alyeska*, which affords a magnificent panoramic 🔽 view of the bay and the mountains. You can either explore the area or have lunch in the panoramic restaurant. Down in the valley you shouldn't miss *Crow Creek Mine*, a picturesque Gold Rush camp dating back to 1898. Panning for gold, you're not likely to find a nugget in your sieve but it's lots

of fun for young and old anyway. Behind the old gold-mine you can take a half-day's hike along a trail to reach Raven Glacier.

Chugach State Park (102/B–C4–5)
Covering an area of 200,000 ha, this vast nature reserve in the glaciers of the Chugach Mountains is right in Anchorage's back yard. The best way to reach it is via *Eagle River* (about 20 km from Anchorage if you drive via Glenn Hwy. and Eagle River Rd.). At the end of the road is the Eagle River Visitor Center (offering exhibitions and nature trails), the starting point for ranger-guided hikes. It also marks the start of a 40-km-long *hiking trail* following the old Iditarod Trail across the mountains to Girdwood – a really rewarding two-day hike.

Eklutna Village (102/B4)
A faithful reconstruction of a mission church dating from the Russian Orthodox missions of 150 years ago is in this small Tanaina Indian village about 40 km northeast of Anchorage. Particularly remarkable: colourful spirit houses, where the souls of the dead are thought to dwell. *In summer daily guided tours 8 am–6 pm, admission $5*

Portage Glacier (102/B5)
★ This is the way you imagine Alaska: glittering icebergs in the foreground against a backdrop of blue waters and green mountains. Gem-like *Portage Lake* at the eastern end of Turnagain Arm is Alaska's most scenic spot. In recent years Portage Glacier has been melting and

calving big icebergs to drift in the little lake.

On the western shore in the *Begich-Boggs Visitor Center (in summer daily 9 am–6 pm, in winter 10 am–4 pm)*, you can see the outstanding film <mark>*Voices from the Ice*</mark> *(admission $1)*.

Alaska Rangers guide you on *nature hikes*, among them an 'Ice-Worm-Safari'. A well-kept 2-km-long *footpath* leads from the car park to Byron Glacier.

A one-hour boat trip will bring you close up to the much bigger ice-field *Portage Glacier*, a truly spectacular sight *(daily 10.30 am–4.30 pm, boat trip $25). About 90 km east of Anchorage on Seward Hwy.*

Turnagain Arm (102/B5)
A 70-km-long fjord south of Anchorage divides the Kenai Peninsula from the mainland. A drive along *Seward Highway* (Hwy. 1), which follows the north shore of the fjord, affords superb views out across the mountains and the tidal flats of this branch of Cook Inlet. Right at the exit leading out of Anchorage, you pass *Potter Marsh*, a bird sanctuary, which is home to many seabirds (nature trails). From the following lookout points, among them *Beluga-Point* about 30 km south of Anchorage, you can sometimes see Beluga whales. Mountain sheep climb precariously on the cliffs. The tidal range in the bay can be up to 10 m – one of the world's highest. Twice a day, for about 2 ½ hours after low tide, waves can get up to 2 m high, so be careful: walks along the sandbanks in Turnagain Arm can be dangerous!

Scenic Alaska

*The South is the most developed region –
and the most beautiful*

Snow-covered mountains and glaciers, remote lakes and forests, bears, eagles and elks – the South abounds in everything you've always imagined Alaska to have in your wildest dreams of the far North. No other region of this vast state unites scenic diversity and variegated fauna so impressively and does it within a scope that is manageable. The region is relatively small and all parts of it are easily accessible. Moreover, the climate is surprisingly temperate here. The sea moderates it considerably so that visitors are delighted to find that summer is often blessed with long, hot sunny days.

The Kenai Peninsula, a mountainous peninsula 200 km long, starts just south of Anchorage. Fjords cut deep into the peninsula's south coast. The interior is full of lakes and salmon streams. Eighty per cent of the peninsula has been turned into nature reserves, but there are still some tiny fishing ports that have remained unchanged since the days before 1867 when the Russians anchored in their harbours.

East of the Kenai Peninsula stretch the fjords and islands of

The Kennicott Mine near McCarthy

spectacular Prince William Sound, fed by the Chugach Mountain glaciers. Pacific winter storms ensure plenty of precipitation in the form of snow so that this mountain chain has more glaciers than are found anywhere else in Alaska. Thompson Pass near Valdez leads Alaska in setting snowfall records. Snow up to 30 m deep has been recorded here. In one day in December 1955 1.6 m of snow fell here – a record that has never been beaten in Alaska!

Southeast Alaska is the state's most highly developed region. Two paved highways run through the Kenai Peninsula, one of them into the interior and the other on to Valdez on the south coasts. The southern region is, therefore, highly suitable for both camping and trips by car. If you book the ferry that runs between Valdez and Whittier early enough, you can even take a round trip. Taken together, the little towns along the road and the numerous, often scenically situated camping sites, represent a highly developed travel infrastructure. Anywhere along the way, you can stop for a canoe trip on the Swanson River, say, or for an excursion into the sublime mountain scenery of Wrangell-St.

Everything for fishermen and hikers: shop for gear in Homer

Elias National Park, the largest nature reserve in the United States.

GLENNALLEN

(**103/D3**) This town (pop. 500) extending along the highway has motels and supermarkets and is the best place in Southeast Alaska for stocking up on supplies. From here *Glenn Highway* runs parallel to the snowy peaks of the Chugach Mountains to Anchorage. Scenic *Richardson Highway* follows the broad Copper River and the Alyeska Pipeline into the mountains to the south before turning north to climb up to Isabel Pass in the Alaska Range.

SURROUNDING AREA

Copper Center (**103/D4**)
This old pioneer town on a sideroad branching off Richardson Hwy. is much more picturesque than modern Glennallen. The historic *Copper Center Lodge* dishes up huge *pancakes* for breakfast and thick juicy steaks for dinner – old-time ambience.

Lake Louise (**103/D3**)
The big wilderness lake northeast of Glennallen is the perfect spot for a peaceful day of summer fun – swimming, camping on the lake shore and a drink in the rustic bar of ✪ Lake Louise Lodge.

HOMER

(**102/A6**) In good weather Homer (pop. 4,200) is breathtakingly beautiful: lofty snow-capped peaks and glaciers encircle the glinting waters of Kachemak Bay. The town is on the north shore. Homer's recent prosperity is due to the abundance of fish in the bay, which makes it a paradise for aficionados of halibut fishing, who leave from *Homer Spit*, a sandbank about 8 km long jutting out into the bay, in charter boats. Everything interesting around here happens on the Spit. Nevertheless, on the mainland it's fun to stroll up *Pioneer Ave.*, which boasts a number of good restaurants and interesting art galleries. Its scenic location has made Homer a mecca for artists. Quite a large artists' colony has settled here. You'll be rewarded with the most beautiful ☀ views out across the broad bay if you go to Skyline Drive and East End Rd.

MUSEUM

Pratt Museum
Pioneer history, ship models, aquariums, exhibitions on fauna – everything you want to know about the region. *3779 Bartlett St., in summer Sun–Wed 10 am–6 pm, Thurs–Sat 10 am–8 pm, admission $4*

RESTAURANTS

Cafe Cups
🏃 Popular with the alternative crowd and known for good food. *162 W Pioneer Ave., Tel. 235 83 30, Category 2–3*

The Saltry
Excellent seafood restaurant in the tiny, ☀ scenic town of Halibut Cove on the south shore of Kachemak Bay. *For reservations call: Tel. 235 78 47, Category 2*

SHOPPING

Ptarmigan Arts
A gallery selling paintings, jewellery, wood sculpture and paintings on silk produced by a 50-member artists' cooperative. *471 E Pioneer Ave.*

ACCOMMODATION

Bay View Inn
Friendly motel on a ☀ high cliff above the bay. *14 rooms, mile 170, Sterling Hwy., Tel. 235 84 85, Fax 235 87 16, Category 2*

Heritage Hotel
Good value. Log-cabin style. *36 rooms, 147 E Pioneer Ave., Tel. 235 77 87, Fax 235 28 04, Category 2*

MARCO POLO SELECTION: SOUTH ALASKA AND THE KENAI PENINSULA

1 Kachemak Bay Lodge
Perfect place to enjoy the wilderness on a remote fjord in Kachemak Bay (page 40)

2 Canoe trips
Paddle your way to the caribou: beginners, too (page 41)

3 McCarthy
Spectacular scenery and a ghost town in America's biggest National Park (pages 46–47)

4 Prince William Sound
Glaciers and fjords, and all topped by the panoramic wilderness (pages 45–46)

5 Salty Dawg Saloon
Worth at least a beer: the region's saltiest saloon (page 40)

6 Seldovia
Boat trips to seabird colonies and a fishing village from the Russian era (page 40)

Kachemak Bay Lodge

★ Classic wilderness lodge for nature-lovers on the south shore of Kachemak Bay. *6 rooms, P.O. Box 956, Homer, AK 99603, Tel. 235 89 10, Fax 235 89 11, incl. all meals, Category 1*

Tutka Bay Lodge

A smoothly run wilderness lodge whose owners are committed to seeing that you enjoy the wilderness with all modern amenities. *4 cabins, P.O. Box 960, Homer, AK 99603, Tel. 235 39 05, Fax 235 39 09, all meals served, Category 1*

SPORTS & LEISURE

Central Charters

Halibut fishing charters and excursions on Kachemak Bay. *On Homer Spit, Tel. 235 78 47*

Homer Ocean Charters

Water taxi and day tours to seabird colonies and bears. *On Homer Spit, Tel. 235 62 12*

ENTERTAINMENT

Salty Dawg Saloon

★ The most famous old-time-style saloon on the Kenai Peninsula: sawdust-strewn floors and life preservers on the walls. *On Homer Spit*

INFORMATION

Homer Chamber of Commerce

Info centre on Sterling Hwy., P.O. Box 541, Homer, AK 99603, Tel. 235 53 00, Fax 235 87 66

SURROUNDING AREA

Seldovia   (102/A6)

★ A beautifully remote, picturesque fishing village on the south shore of Kachemak Bay, it was founded in 1795 by the Russians. Well worth a day trip but you can also spend the night in the Boardwalk Hotel *(14 rooms, Tel. 234 78 16, Category 2).* Tours and ferry service with the *Danny J: Tel. 235 78 48*

HOPE

(102/B5) This historic Gold Rush town on the south coast of Turnagain Arm still looks rather wild and rakish. The population of what might almost be termed a ghost town has grown again from 15 to 250, but there are still plenty of Wild West façades and derelict houses for nostalgic holiday snapshots.

SPORTS & LEISURE

Resurrection Pass Trail

The most famous and by far the most scenic hiking trail in Chugach National Forest starts at Hope. It runs south for 61 km to Cooper Landing on the Kenai River past lots of lakes full of fish, waterfalls and derelict trappers' cabins. *Info and cabin bookings in the Alaska Public Lands Information Centre in Anchorage*

KENAI/SOLDOTNA

(102/A–B5) This modern, sprawling double town (pop. 11,000) on the mouth of the Kenai River in Cook Inlet in the heart of the oil country is now a favourite among salmon fishers. The only reminder that Kenai was founded in 1791 by Russian fur traders is the onion-domed *Holy Assumption Church (guided tours)* on a high bluff above the river mouth. From the vantage-point of nearby ⚜ *Beluga Lookout* you can see far across Cook Inlet to the volcanoes marking the beginning of the Aleutian Island chain.

ACCOMMODATION

Longmere Lake B & B
Big log cabin, scenic lakeside location. *6 rooms, P.O. Box 1707, Soldotna, AK 99669, Tel. 262 97 99, Fax 262 59 37, Category 2*

Posey's Kenai River Hideaway
Cosy B & B lodge for salmon fishing on the Kenai River. *5 rooms, P.O. Box 4094, Soldotna, AK 99669, Tel. and Fax 262 74 30, Category 1–2*

SPORTS & LEISURE

Alaska Wildland Adventures
Specialists in white-water rafting tours on the Kenai River and wilderness trips, also to other Alaskan regions. *Mile 50.1, Cooper Landing. Postal address: P.O. Box 389, Girdwood, AK 99587, Tel. 783 29 28, Fax 783 21 30*

Fishing
More than 40,000 king salmon – some of them record-breaking whoppers – are caught every year by fishers in the fabulous Kenai River. The most coveted spots are near Cooper Landing and at the confluence of the Russian and Kenai rivers. Lots of tackle shops (fishing gear) and fishing lodges in and near Soldotna sell fishing licences and arrange for guides.

Canoe trips
The long chain of lakes in Kenai National Wildlife Refuge north of Sterling Highway has two ★ *wilderness canoe routes*, which are suitable for beginners, too: the Swan Lake Route (90 km) and the Swanson River Trail (140 km). There are several shops with canoes and equipment for hire in Soldotna.

INFORMATION

Kenai Visitors' Center
Info centre and museum. *11471 Kenai Spur Hwy., Kenai, AK 99611, Tel. 283 19 91, Fax 283 22 30*

Primeval rock and ice: Kenai Fjords National Park

Kenai National Wildlife Refuge Center

A large information agency with natural history exhibitions and videos. Here you can find out everything about canoeing and hiking trips. *Soldotna, Ski Hill Rd., Tel. 262 70 21, Fax 262 35 99*

PALMER

(102/B4) Palmer (pop. 4,300) is the hub of the fertile Matanuska Valley, which is Alaska's most important farming region. This is the place to admire the local 'super produce' in market gardens. Since there are so many long, sunny days in summer here, cabbages grow into behemoths weighing up to 30 kg. Even if everything in Anchorage is booked up in high season, you may still be able to find accommodation in the many motels and camping sites in nearby Palmer.

MUSEUM

Iditarod Trail Committee

Exhibitions dealing with the legendary dog-sled race. *Mile 2.2, Knik Rd., in summer daily 8 am– 5 pm, admission free*

SURROUNDING AREA

Hatcher Pass Road   (102/B4)

A tortuous dirt road from Palmer to Willow on Parks Highway is nerve-racking, but worth it for ↘↙ fabulous views of the Chugach Mountains and of the haunting ruins from Gold Rush days, such as *Independence Mine.*

Matanuska Glacier   (102/C4)

Down in a deep gorge the ↘↙ Glenn Highway follows the Matanuska River for about 100 km to its source, the majestic, gleaming white Matanuska Glacier. You can climb right up on the glacier via a private road in Glacier Park Resort.

SEWARD

(102/B5) The only port city on the south coast of the Kenai Peninsula is typical of South Alaska: encircled by green mountains and right up on a bay, which still yields plentiful harvests of fish. About 3,000 people make their living fishing salmon and halibut, working in port and in railway goods transport and, increasingly, in tourism, which has been booming since the nearby Kenai Fjords National Park was opened in 1980.

Resurrection Bay, with Seward nestled on the mountain slopes at its end, is a fjord discovered 200 years ago by the Russians. Although it is ice-free year round, this natural harbour was not used until the Alaska Railroad was constructed from here into the interior in 1903. The city grew around the train station. Patriotically, it bears the name of William Seward, the American Secretary of State who negotiated the purchase of Alaska from the Russians in 1867. The port is mainly used for shipping coal to Korea.

SIGHTS

The most bustling part of the town is around *Small Boat Harbor,* but the little downtown section around 4th Ave., which has retained something of its pioneer ambience, is well worth a stroll. At the *corner of Jefferson Ave. and 3rd Ave.*, the little *Resurrection Bay Historical Society Museum* houses exhibitions dealing with civic history and the famous Iditarod Trail. Just a short distance away in *St. Peter's Episcopal Church (2nd Ave./Adams St.)*, you can see a mural, which has transplanted the Resurrection to Seward Bay.

MUSEUM

Alaska SeaLife Center
A spacious modern exhibition centre and aquarium, which shows the underwater world of the fjords. *301 Railway Ave., in summer daily 8 am–8 pm, admission $12.50*

RESTAURANTS

Apollo
⚘ Greco-Italian cuisine and, naturally, seafood. *4th Ave., Tel. 224 30 92, Category 2–3*

Ray's
Good seafood restaurant with a ⚘ lovely harbour view. *On Small Boat Harbor, Tel. 224 56 06, Category 2*

ACCOMMODATION

Creekside Cabins
Four cosy log cabins. Right in the woods, quiet. Sauna and camping. *Glacier Rd. exit, Tel. 224 38 34, Category 3*

Harborview Inn
A very comfortable and modern motel, which is not far from the harbour. *13 rooms, 804 3rd Ave., Tel. 224 32 17, Fax 224 32 18, Category 2*

SPORTS & LEISURE

Kayak Adventures
This is where you can book day and longer trips by kayak on Seward Bay and in Kenai Fjords National Park. *414 K St., Anchorage, Tel. 258 38 60*

Hiking
At Jefferson St. begins the 5-km-long trail to *Mt. Marathon,* where an annual 4th of July foot race is held for participants from across Alaska. A second trail is 7 km longer, *Caines Head*, with a lovely view across fjords and islands. Two longer routes recommended are *Lost Lake Trail* and the *Primrose Trail* through the lake country north of Seward and the 34-km-long *Johnson Pass Trail. Information and trail maps for hiking in the whole region are available from the Forest Service, 334 4th Ave., Tel. 224 33 74*

INFORMATION

Seward Visitors' Bureau
Information bureau on Seward Hwy. *P. O. Box 749, Seward, AK 99664, Tel. 224 80 51, Fax 224 53 53*

SURROUNDING AREA

Kenai Fjords National Park   (102/B5-6)
Covering an area of 2,790 km², the park protects a fjordscape carved by the movement of glaciers on the southeastern Kenai Peninsula and is the habitat of marine mammals, such as whales, otters and walruses. The interior of the park also includes the 1850 km² of the *Harding Icefield,* from which numerous glaciers flow imperceptibly into

the sea. The *Visitors' Center* of the Park (slide- and video shows) is situated on Small Boat Harbor in Seward. From here you can start out on half-day and day *sightseeing trips to the glacier inlets.* Book at *Kenai Fjords Tours (Tel. 224 80 68)* or *Mariah Tours (Tel. 224 86 23).* Fed by the Harding Icefield, the *Exit Glacier* can be reached by car via Seward Highway. At the end of Exit Glacier Road, you can take a short footpath that leads right up to the edge of the glacier.

Seward Highway (102/B5)

Running straight through the mountains of the Kenai Peninsula, this highway links Seward with Anchorage, 200 km away. The southern end of the highway around *Trail Lake* and *Kenai Lake* is dotted with superb ✿ look-out points, little lodges and camping sites.

VALDEZ

(**103/D4**) 'Alaska's Switzerland' is what Valdez (pop. 4,000) likes to be called and the region does bear comparison with its namesake. Of course the town is right on the sea. It is the gateway to Prince William Sound, but the mountain peaks and glaciers encircling it are magnificently Alpine. Founded in the late 19th century, Valdez was the port of call for gold prospectors leaving for the interior. Unfortunately, nothing is left of old Valdez. A tidal wave caused by the 1964 earthquake destroyed it.

Life in Valdez revolves around *Small Boat Harbor*: restaurants and shops line North Harbor

Seals in Prince William Sound

Drive. Sightseeing boats dock in front. Across from it, on the eastern shore of Valdez Fjord, the huge tanks of the oil terminals are visible, which mark the *end of the Alyeska Pipeline (to book guided tours: Tel. 835 2686)*. The oil spill has made Valdez notorious worldwide for being the site of Alaska's biggest oil catastrophe: in 1989 the supertanker *Exxon Valdez* struck Bligh Reef at the harbour mouth. Forty-two million litres of crude oil flowed into the Gulf of Alaska, polluting the shoreline as far away as Kodiak Island. By now the oil has become invisible, at least to the naked eye, and even the fauna seems to have recovered from its effects. Sea otters frolic in the headwaters of the bay and silver salmon are again thronging to it to spawn in August near the city.

MUSEUM

Valdez Museum
Small but interesting, on pioneer history. Exhibitions dealing with the 1964 earthquake and the oil disaster. *217 Egan Drive, in summer daily 9 am–6 pm, admission $3*

RESTAURANT

Mike's Palace
Always packed and deservedly so: pizza, seafood and Mexican food. *201 N Harbor Drive, Tel. 835 23 65, Category 2*

ACCOMMODATION

Downtown B & B inn
Big downtown inn. *25 rooms, 113 Galena Drive, Tel. 835 27 91, Fax 835 54 06, Category 2*

SPORTS & LEISURE

Anadyr Adventures
Kayaks for hire and guided tours to glacier fjords near Valdez. *Office on the port: P.O. Box 1821, Valdez, AK 99686, Tel. and Fax 835 28 14*

ENTERTAINMENT

Harbor Club Bar
❀ Popular among fishermen. Live music at weekends. *205 N Harbor Drive*

INFORMATION

Valdez Visitors' Bureau
200 Chenega St., Valdez, AK 99686, Tel. 835 29 84, Fax 835 48 45

SURROUNDING AREA

Cordova (103/D5)
A pretty, remote fishing village at the eastern end of Prince William Sound, popular among nature-lovers for being the starting point of tours to the ◣ *Copper River delta*. In spring millions of migratory birds gather here. Trumpeter swans and many other species of waterfowl nest in the wetlands in summer.

Prince William Sound (102–103/C–D4)
★ Whales and seals, icebergs, islands and spectacular fjords: covering nearly 40,000 km², the sound at the foot of the Chugach Mountains represents Alaska at its most beautiful. The most celebrated sight here is the (approx. 40,000 km²) *Columbia Glacier*, which in recent years has shrunk by nearly 10 km.

Sightseeing tours from Valdez with Prince William Sound Cruises, Tel. 835 47 31

Richardson Highway   (102–103/C–D1–3)
As early as 1910, the first wagon trail in Alaska was built from Valdez through the mountains to Fairbanks, the magnificent ◀▶ Richardson Highway. From Valdez you first drive through marvellous, waterfall-fringed *Keystone Canyon*, and then the road rises to heights with views of the *Chugach Mountains*. At ◀▶ *Thompson Pass* (845 m) the glittering ablation zone of *Worthington Glacier* extends almost to the road.

WHITTIER

(102/C5) Whittier is not scenic but unusual. Almost the entire population of 300 souls is quartered in a few rambling military buildings left over from World War II, when the little port town was an important army base. Nowadays Whittier is 'civilized' as the western gateway to the wonderland of ★ *Prince William Sound*. Tour boats taking visitors to superb *College Fjord* depart from Whittier harbour. This is where you leave for camping tours through the labyrinth of islands, and hikers can take the *Portage Pass Trail* for scenic half-day walks to the glaciers high above town.

Incidentally, the settlement is not accessible by car. The *Alaska Railroad* takes you and your car piggyback from the Seward Highway near Portage to Whittier. From there a *ferry* crosses the Sound to Valdez three times a week (reservations with *Alaska Marine Highway* absolutely necessary!). This is also a great place to leave your car behind and take a boat trip or simply go hiking.

Phillips Cruises
Six-hour sightseeing tours in a big catamaran. Departure from Whittier harbour. *Book in advance: 519 W 4th Ave., Anchorage, Tel. 276 80 23*

Trail & Sail Adventures
Half- and full-day kayak and sailing trips throughout Prince William Sound. *10801 Trails End Rd., Anchorage, Tel. and Fax 276 26 28*

WRANGELL-ST. ELIAS NATIONAL PARK/ McCARTHY

(103/D–F3–6, 104/A–B5–6) A national park that is bigger than Switzerland! The 50,000 km² wilderness encompasses volcanoes and icefields, such as *Bagley Icefield*, from which the 160-km long *Bering Glacier* flows. From scenic ◀▶ *Richardson Highway* you can see peaks like lofty *Mt. Sanford* (4,949 m). At the icy heart of the park, peaks such as *Mt. Saint Elias* soar up to 5,500 m. Together with neighbouring *Kluane National Park* in Canada, this completely undeveloped wilderness area, established as a nature reserve in 1980, has been declared a UNESCO Natural Heritage Site.

The park is only accessible via two roads: a 70-km-long *dirt*

Highways of ice: glaciers in Wrangell-St. Elias National Park

track from Nabesna in the north and, superbly scenic, 150-km-long  *McCarthy Road,* which runs from Richardson Highway to the weather-beaten ★ mining town of *McCarthy.* You should leave your car at the end of the road, which is due to be resurfaced, by the Kennicott River and then walk on to the town or another 5 km to the huge *Kennicott Mine,* which sprawls in the wilderness, abandoned to all comers.

ACCOMMODATION

Kennicott Glacier Lodge
The view from the veranda across the Kennicott Glacier is incomparable. *25 rooms. Postal address: P.O. Box 103940, Anchorage, AK 99510, Tel. 258 23 50, Fax 248 79 75, Category 1*

McCarthy Lodge
Historic hotel in McCarthy. Restaurant, saloon, backpacker hostelry. *12 rooms, P.O. Box MXY, Glennallen, AK 99588, Tel. 554 44 02, Fax 554 44 04, Category 2*

SPORTS & LEISURE

Copper Oar
Wilderness Alaska: trips on inflatable rubber dinghies on the Copper River, which take several days. Mountain-bike hire and mountaineering guides. *In the old McCarthy power station, P.O. Box MXY, McCarthy, Glennallen, AK 99588, Tel. and Fax 554 44 53*

Wrangell Mountain Air
Circle above the glaciers. Transport service for hikers. *McCarthy, Tel. 554 44 00*

INFORMATION

Wrangell-St. Elias National Park
Info centres in Copper Center and Chitina. *Postal address: P.O. Box 439, Copper Center, AK 99573, Tel. 822 52 34, Fax 822 72 16*

The highest peak and the biggest river

*The country between the Yukon River
and the white peaks of the Alaska Range is vast*

From afar Mt. McKinley dominates the interior of Alaska. The state's tallest mountain, it is also its grandest. In solitary splendour its icy cone looks ethereal on clear days against the backdrop of the green foothills of the Alaska Range, visible for 100 or even 200 km away. Denali, 'the Lofty One', is its Indian name. Nowadays interest groups are trying to give the mountain back the name the indigenous peoples of Alaska called it. The national park around it has recently been renamed Denali. A gold prospector named the peak after William McKinley, who was then presidential candidate, without knowing all that much about its local history.

The interior includes the Alaska Range and the broad (at least 500 km) valley of the Yukon River and its tributaries. The state's biggest river flows 3,185 km from its modest source in the Coast Mountains of the Canadian Yukon Territory across the North Slope of the continent to the Bering Sea. Low chains of hills bisect the Yukon Valley. In autumn endless murmuring woods of birch and aspen glow with orange and yellow leaves during the last warm days of the year.

The most wonderful thing about the Alaskan interior is, in fact, its summer climate. Protected by the high barrier of the Alaska Range, it has little rainfall. In summer temperatures often rise to above 30°C (86°F). Winter is another kettle of fish altogether: the interior is then the coldest region of Alaska. In January and February, when the Aurora Borealis is flickering in spectacular displays of coloured light across the sky, the temperature is likely to remain at –40°C (–40°F) for icy weeks on end.

The harsh winters are probably what deterred settlers from remaining here. Despite the Gold Rush at the turn of the century, the region has remained largely unpopulated. One city, a dozen towns – that's all you'll find in a region about the size of Great Britain.

There are, however, a few highways that bisect the broad country of the interior, some of

Autumn foliage on the Denali Highway – the trees turn colour in Alaska by mid-September

49

MARCO POLO SELECTION: CENTRAL ALASKA AND FAIRBANKS

1 Denali Park Road
Scenic highway with superb views of Mt. McKinley (page 51)

2 K2 Aviation
Classic flight over the highest peak in North America, Mt. McKinley (page 55)

3 Santa Claus House
Christmas in summer: kitsch galore, but lots of fun (page 55)

4 University Museum Fairbanks
Gold, mammoth tusks and a 36,000-year-old steppe bison (page 53)

them leading to small back-country pioneer towns, others to wilderness camping sites and hiking country on remote, quiet forest lakes and hot springs, where tired gold prospectors once soaked the weariness out of their aching bones.

DELTA JUNCTION

(**103/D2**) Mile 1,422, Alaska Highway: *the end of the road*. For at least 50 years Delta Junction (pop. 700) has been the goal of overland travellers on the legendary Alaska Highway, which starts far down south in Canada at Dawson Creek. At the centre of this village straggling along the highway, in front of the Visitor Centre, stands the official last *milestone* of the military road built in 1942. From here, then as now, Richardson Highway goes on to Fairbanks and Valdez in the south. Delta Junction is the only farming town in the interior. About 15,000 ha of land have been cleared in the past 20 years. The main cereal crops cultivated here are oats, wheat and other grains.

SIGHTS

Big Delta State Historical Park (**103/D1**)
The perfect picture: a little museum village with a lovingly restored stagecoach station dating from 1910: *Rika's Roadhouse.* Just to the north of it, the ✺ *Alyeska Pipeline* crosses the Tanana River in a gleaming arch. *Mile 275, Richardson Hwy., in summer daily 8 am–8 pm, admission free*

DENALI NATIONAL PARK

(**102/A–B2-3**) In 1980 the Park (founded in 1917) was enlarged. Now this wilderness region covers 24,395 km², an area larger than Wales. Its main attraction is *Mt. McKinley*, at 6,194 m the highest peak in North America. However, what makes a visit most rewarding is the *animal life*. In summer the tundra is embroidered with wild flowers. This is the habitat of about 2,000 elk, 3,000 caribou and nearly 300 grizzly bears as well as mountain sheep, foxes, wolves, eagles and many other northern species. Since most of the nature reserve is above the timber line and hunting is strictly forbidden, you are likely to spot some of its residents, which are not afraid of people.

Blocked off for through traffic, ★ *Denali Park Road* runs from the entrance to the park along the north slope of the Alaska Range for 135 km into the interior of the nature reserve, where you can stop at the *Eielson Visitor Center* and *Wonder Lake* to enjoy the most superb ◁⊳ views of the lonely mountain. You can also request your bus driver to let you off at the park and then take a later bus back. If you want to hike off into the back country for several days, you are required to enter your name at the Backcountry Desk in the Visitor Centre. In peak season you may have to wait a day or two for a seat on the bus. If so, why not take a detour on the *Denali Highway*, go rafting on the *Nenana River* or pay a visit to the *sled dogs* owned by the Park Rangers *(daily guided tours of the dog kennels in the park headquarters)* while you're waiting.

TOURS

★ Bus trips along the Denali Park Road leave from the entrance to the park at the Visitor Centre. Tickets for bus trips are issued there up to three days ahead. Some of the seats can be reserved six months in advance. *Tel. 272 72 75, Fax 264 46 84, tickets $12.50–$31, depending on the route desired.*

RESTAURANTS

Denali Dining Room
Hearty American home cooking in the historic railroad hotel at the park entrance. In the evening the ✪ Golden Spike Saloon in two old Alaska Railroad carriages is a favourite. *Tel. 276 72 34, Category 2–3*

The Perch
Good steaks and seafood with a ◁⊳ view across the Nenana Valley. *Mile 224, Parks Hwy., Tel. 683 25 23, Category 2*

ACCOMMODATION

Camp Denali
Simple log cabins with running cold water, at the heart of the park. ◁⊳ Superb view of the mountain. Guided nature walks. Book well in advance! *Postal address: P.O. Box 67, Denali National Park, AK 99755, Tel. 683 22 90, Fax 683 15 68, incl. three meals, Category 1*

Denali Grizzly Bear Cabins
Eight simple but modern log cabins south of the park entrance. Camping site. *Mile 231, Parks Hwy., Tel. 683 26 96, Category 2*

Denali Dome Home B & B
Friendly B & B north of the park entrance. *9 rooms, P.O. Box 262, Healy, AK 99743, Tel. 683 12 39, Fax 683 23 22, Category 2*

Denali Hostel
⋏ Simple backpacker hostel on the northern fringe of the park. Shuttle service to Park entrance. *30 beds, P.O. Box 801, Denali Park, Tel. 683 12 95, Category 3*

Scanty pickings: caribou in Denali National Park

Kantishna Roadhouse
Comfortable wilderness lodge at the end of the Park road. Good hiking trails close by. *28 rooms, P.O. Box 130, Denali National Park, AK 99755, Tel. 479 24 36, Fax 479 26 11, incl. three meals, Category 1*

INFORMATION

Denali National Park
Big info centre on your right at park entrance. Sign in here for the seven camping sites in the Park. *P.O. Box 9, McKinley Park, AK 99755, Tel. 683 22 94, Fax 683 96 11*

EAGLE

(103/F1) A long, bumpy drive on a road branching off the Taylor Hwy. to follow the bank of the Yukon River shouldn't deter you from visiting this romantic gold prospector settlement. Guided tours every morning through the exhibitions in the *Court House* (1901) and the old *Customs House* as well as partly restored *Fort Egbert,* built by the US Army in 1899, tell you all about the heady pioneer days. From here the earliest gold prospectors set out for the Klondike and the big Yukon steamers left for the Bering Sea. After the boom era early this century, only 150 souls were left in the settlement and the population has not increased.

Wilderness fans can set out down the Yukon and paddle through *Yukon-Charley Rivers National Preserve* as far as Circle *(information in the Park Visitor Center in Eagle).*

FAIRBANKS

☞ City Map inside back cover

(102/C1) Nowadays Fairbanks (pop. 85,000) plays second fiddle to Anchorage. However, from the early Gold Rush boom years of the 20th century until long after World War II, it was Alaska's principal city. Even now Fairbanks is the supply hub for Central Alaska and the Arctic region.

The vast Prudhoe Bay oil fields were developed from Fairbanks. Bush pilots take off from here to the back country to shuttle supplies to Inuit settlements and set geologists, gold prospectors, rafters and hikers down in the wilderness.

A rather shady merchant, one Captain Barnette, founded a small trading post on the bank of the Chena River in 1901. When gold was discovered nearby a year later, the settlement's future was assured.

Gold prospectors flocked into the region (and you'll still see them scratching around in them thar hills north of Fairbanks). By 1917 the town had a university. In 1923 came the railroad, during World War II the US Army and in the 1970s the oil boom – a steady economic upturn.

With its jumble of old cabins, new office tower blocks and broad streets lined with billboards, this is not a lovely looking city but it is typically Alaskan. You should take at least a day to see it: downtown around *Cushman Street* there are some things to look at – like the tiny *Ice Museum* in an old cinema *(500 2nd Ave.)* – and you should stock up on supplies here before taking off for the back country.

SIGHTS

Alaskaland
Fairground and open-air museum in one: picturesque pioneer houses, shops, an old paddle-wheel steamer, Salmon Bake (a salmon barbecue picnic), gold-prospecting equipment and a saloon (shows in the evening). *Airport Way, in summer daily 11 am– 9 pm, admission free*

Gold Dredge No. 8
Right out in the historic Gold District north of Fairbanks, you can take a guided tour through this huge old gold dredge and learn everything about gold mining. Afterwards you can try your luck at panning. On the way you will pass the Alyeska Pipeline. *Mile 9, Old Steese Hwy., in summer daily 9 am–6 pm, admission $19.50*

Riverboat Discovery
Half-day trips in a paddle-wheel steamer on the Chena and the Tanana rivers. *Dock at the western end of Airport Way, to book steamer trips: Tel. 479 66 73, tickets $40*

MUSEUM

University Museum
★ In a lovely setting on a hill above the city, this modern museum gives an outstanding survey of Alaskan natural and pioneer history. *Right on the University of Fairbanks campus, in summer daily 9 am–7 pm, admission $5*

TOURS

Frontier Flying Service
Excursions by plane to Nome, Kotzebue and into Gates of the Arctic National Park. *3820 University Ave., Tel. 474 00 14*

RESTAURANTS

Ester Gold Camp
Touristy but lots of fun: you can eat your fill at the halibut buffet in the old gold-prospectors' camp and then tank up in the *Malemute Saloon* (evening shows). *15 min. west on Parks Hwy., Tel. 479 25 00, Category 2–3*

Monument to Native Americans: the 'First Family' in Fairbanks

Pike's Landing
❖ Steaks, seafood and good beer. Riverside terrace. Very good Sunday brunch. *Mile 4.5, Airport Way, Tel. 479 71 13, Category 2–3*

You will find many large shopping malls along University Ave. and on Old Steese Highway. Sporting-goods centres and camping equipment stores as well as art galleries and souvenir shops are mostly to be found downtown at Cushman Ave. and 2nd Ave.

ACCOMMODATION

B & B Reservation Service
Agency for about 50 B & B inns throughout the city. *763 7th Ave., Fairbanks, Tel. 479 81 65, Fax 474 84 48, Category 1–2*

Bridgewater
Comfortable family hotel, downtown. *94 rooms, 723 1st Ave., Tel. 452 66 61, Fax 452 61 26, Category 2*

INFORMATION

Fairbanks Visitor Center
550 First Ave., Fairbanks, AK 99701, Tel. 456 57 74, Fax 452 28 67

SURROUNDING AREA

Dalton Highway   (100/A1–6)
Not inaugurated until 1944, the pipeline highway runs for 666 lonely kilometres through the Brooks Range to Prudhoe Bay on the Arctic Ocean. The last stretch has never been open to the public; you can only visit the central oil processing facility by taking a guided tour. *The Northern Alaska Tour Company (Tel. 474 86 00, Fax 474 47 67) offers tours leaving from Fairbanks*

Hot Springs   (100/B6)
It's well worth your while to take side-roads out from Fairbanks into the back country: only an hour's drive away is *Chena Hot Springs*, a resort hotel *(76 rooms, Tel. 452 78 67, Fax 456 31 22, Category 2)* with hot springs. It's about 200 km to *Circle Hot Springs* (a fine building,

24 rooms, 10 cabins, Tel. 520 51 13, Fax 520 54 42, Category 2–3), where early 20th-century gold prospectors soaked in the hot springs for rest and relaxation.

North Pole (102/C1)
Father Christmas dwells at the North Pole so many American children send their Christmas lists to Santa Claus at North Pole, Alaska. The ★ *Santa Claus House* in this Fairbanks suburb is Christmasy all year round with strains of 'Jingle Bells' ringing out in July. *25 km to the east on Richardson Hwy.*

NENANA

(102/C1) This small town (pop. 500) at the confluence of the Nenana and the broad Tanana rivers grew out of a Dena Indian settlement after the railway came here in 1923. The *Alaska Railroad Museum (in summer daily 9 am–6 pm)* in the beautifully restored train station on the river bank sheds light on that era. In summer you're likely to see Native American fish wheels, like little paddle-wheel steamers, scooping up salmon from the Tanana River. The town is also renowned throughout Alaska for its *Ice Classic,* a lottery based on guessing exactly when the ice will start to break up into floes in the river. Every Alaskan plays: the jackpot is worth $250,000.

TALKEETNA

(102/B3) Somehow time has stood still in Talkeetna (pop. 400) for 30 years. The pioneer spirit hovers over the old log cabins and Western façades, and Main St. is still the only paved road in town. Talkeetna is south of the Alaska Range, yet to mountaineers it represents the *gateway to Mt. McKinley.* Its proximity to the Arctic Circle has left it covered with glaciers, making it a supreme test of mountaineering prowess in international climbing. Many a climber lies buried in the cemetery next to the airport. In bars like the ☗ *Swiss-Alaska Inn,* climbers meet to talk shop before they are flown out by K2 Aviation to storm the peak from Base Camp. *Tel. 733 22 91, also ★ sightseeing flights over the mountain*

ACCOMMODATION

Three Rivers B & B
Arranges private rooms and cosy log cabins. *P.O. Box 525, Talkeetna, AK 99676, Tel. and Fax 733 27 41, Category 2*

INFORMATION

Talkeetna Ranger Station
Advice and information for climbers who want to venture up Mt. McKinley. *P.O. Box 588, Talkeetna, AK 99676, Tel. 733 22 31, no Fax*

TOK

(103/E2) Tok (pop. 1,200) seems to consist of nothing but filling stations and motels – not surprisingly, as this is the first Alaskan town you reach if you come from the south on the Alaska Highway. After the wilderness of the Canadian Yukon Territory, 'civilization' starts here. Two big Information Centres help you plan the rest of your trip.

Land of fjords and forests

*Explore Southeast Alaska's labyrinth
of islands by ship*

The American naturalist and philosopher John Muir raved about the 'solitude of ice and newborn rocks, dim, dreary, mysterious' a century ago when he was exploring Glacier Bay. This spectacular bay, created by meltwater from the glaciers surrounding it on the northern fringe of the Alaska Panhhandle has remained one of Alaska's major attractions: a primeval realm of calving glaciers, drift ice and glittering white snowy peaks rising to nearly 5,000 m.

For all the glacial splendour in the north, the Panhandle does not match the clichés of Alaska as the land of the Inuit and polar bears. Its colours are the deep green of coniferous forests and the blue of the sea. Fishing villages and small Tlingit Indian setttlements add splashes of colour, scattered about in the labyrinth of thickly wooded islands and fjords. Humpback whales and seals swim in the bays. Rendered temperate by the sea, the climate is mild here – and damp. Clouds

that have built up over the Pacific dump their precipitation on the western slopes of the Coast Mountains, creating the best possible conditions for a unique 'northern' rainforest, where Sitka spruce and Douglas firs grow to be centuries old and ferns and moss are omnipresent.

Southeast Alaska is, therefore, not Arctic, as you might expect it to be. Ketchikan, its southernmost town, is on the latitude of Copenhagen. Juneau, the capital of Alaska, is more southerly than Stockholm. Alaskans call this region the Panhandle because it looks as if it had been attached to the continent like the handle of a saucepan. Most of the region is now part of Tongass National Forest (approx. 7 million ha). Comprising numerous specially protected wilderness areas, it is an ideal place for kayaking enthusiasts and lovers of the wilderness. Even today only three Panhandle towns – Hyder, Haines and Skagway – are linked with the outside world by road. This does not mean, however, that the region has no infrastructure. Salmon fisheries and loggers have been at work here since the late 19th cen-

*Shades of green:
Juneau, Alaska's capital*

tury and have founded a great many towns. The whole region is dotted with fishing and wilderness lodges. From 1896 goldseekers took the celebrated Inside Passages, a protected waterway that wends its way through the islands and fjords fringing the Panhandle, to reach the goldfields of the Klondike in the Yukon.

The Inside Passage is still the most beautiful gateway to exploring the magnificent skerries of Southeast Alaska. You can either travel in luxury on a cruise ship or on your own on one of the large state-owned car ferries operated by the Alaska Marine Highway (be sure to book well in advance!). Plan to stop at several of the coastal towns and take a kayak trip or spend a few days in a lodge or cabin. Whatever time of year you go, don't forget your rain gear!

GLACIER BAY NATIONAL PARK/ GUSTAVUS

(108/A–B2) On a beautiful ☙ boat trip through Glacier Bay, a fjord roughly 110 km long, you'll find all your dreams of Alaska come true: dramatic walls of ice, steep fjords, drift ice with seals dozing on it and, if you're lucky, even humpback whales sounding from the deep against a breathtakingly beautiful backdrop. Ten glaciers feed into the bay, which has many

MARCO POLO SELECTION: SOUTHEAST ALASKA AND THE PANHANDLE

1 Alaska Discovery Expeditions
Simply the best wilderness trips: hiking, rafting or kayaking (page 62)

2 The Alaskan Hotel bar
A traditional saloon: rough, dark and loud (page 61)

3 Chilkoot Trail
In the footsteps of the gold prospectors (page 70)

4 Gastineau Salmon Hatchery
All you ever wanted to know about the life of salmon (page 61)

5 Glacier Bay Country Inn
Wilderness in comfort: an elegant lodge on Glacier Bay (page 59)

6 Misty Fjords National Monument
Fjords, eagles and waterfalls: a natural wonderland (pages 65–66)

7 Sheldon Jackson Museum
Superb collections of artefacts made by Native Americans and the Inuit (page 68)

8 Totem Bight Historical Park
This is Alaska: totem poles, sea and forests (page 64)

Glacier Bay National Park: Southeast Alaska at its most spectacular

arms. Above it rears the sublime peak of *Mt. Fairweather* (4,663 m). It is incredible but true that this huge bay did not exist 207 years ago. In 1792, when Captain Vancouver sailed past, it was still covered by a layer of ice 1,200 m thick. Since that time the mighty glaciers have receded. Forests and wild flowers have clothed what were then naked rocky slopes. Bears and more than 200 species of bird are now native to the region. Any tour you might take into the vast nature reserve (approx. 13,000 km²), which was established in 1925, starts out from the town of Gustavus on the southern entrance to the bay (ferry link from Juneau).

region. For stays book with *Glacier Bay Lodge (56 rooms, Category 1–2)*, the only accommodation available in the park, with a small backpackers' hostel. *Postal address: 520 Pike St., Seattle, WA 98101, Tel. 206/623 24 17, Fax 623 78 09*

ACCOMMODATION

Annie Mae Lodge
Cosy, welcoming lodge with ten rooms at the 🏷 southern entrance to the Bay. *P.O. Box 80, Gustavus, Tel. 697 23 46, Fax 697 22 11, incl. three meals, Category 1–2*

Glacier Bay Country Inn
★ Very comfortable lodge with superb food. Also offers a wide selection of tours. *9 rooms, Gustavus, P.O. Box 5, Tel. 697 22 88, Fax 697 22 89, incl. three meals, Category 1*

TOURS

Glacier Bay Tours
Full-day excursions by boat in the park leaving from Bartlett Cove and whale-watching trips. Also a broad selection of longer tours (and kayaking trips) in the entire

The Growley Bear
Modern B & B in town. Unpretentious, pleasant and clean. *5 rooms, P.O. Box 246, Gustavus, Tel. 697 27 30, Category 2*

Glacier Bay Sea Kayaks

Kayaks for hire if you want to spend several days touring the Bay. *P.O. Box 26, Gustavus, Tel. 697 22 57, Fax 697 30 02*

Glacier Bay National Park

Bartlett Cove, Gustavus, AK 99826, Tel. 697 22 30, Fax 697 26 54

HAINES

(108/B2) In recent years the American bald eagle has brought fame to this old Tlingit settlement and fishing port in the northern Panhandle. Every year about 4,000 *bald eagles* gather in late autumn in the Chilkat River Valley to feast on the last of the salmon, a magnificent sight for bird-watchers and photographers. All year round the town (pop. 1,200) is an attractive place, set against the dramatic backdrop of the Coast Mountains. Quite a few bald eagles stay there all summer. You can take Haines as your starting-point for trips to nearby ⇖ *Chilkoot Lake* (camping site), where you can go canoeing, swimming and salmon fishing.

The little *Sheldon Museum (in summer daily 1 pm–5 pm)* at the top of Main St. preserves the cultural legacy of the Tlingit Indians: ancient totem poles and beautifully woven blankets of mountain-goat wool. Several charter companies like the *L.A.B. Flying Service (Tel. 766 22 22)* arrange *sightseeing flights for individuals or groups* across Glacier Bay. In addition, the town of Haines is on the most direct route to the North, via scenic *Haines Highway*, which feeds into the *Alaska Highway* It will take you two or three days of driving to reach Fairbanks or Anchorage.

Fort William H. Seward

Founded as an army post in 1904, the fort is now a protected historic monument. The little houses in which the officers were quartered have been restored. Now they house restaurants and culture centres. The Chilkat Dancers, a Tlingit dance group, perform Native American dances. *Information: Tel. 766 20 00, admission free, performance $10*

Fort Seward Lodge

Steaks and fresh crab, with a ⇖ view across the harbour and the mountains. Has a bar and an unpretentious *motel (10 rooms)* as well. *Fort Seward, Tel. 766 20 09, Fax 766 20 06, Category 2*

Chilkat Center for the Arts

You can watch Native Americans at work carving in several workshops and buy the finished artefacts: masks, fine wooden bowls or even an authentic carved totem pole – for $5,000. *In Fort Seward*

Fort Seward B & B

A friendly and cosy B & B in the house which was once allocated to the Fort Seward regimental doctor. *7 rooms, P.O. Box 5, Tel. 766 28 56, Category 2–3*

Hälsingland Hotel
A beautifully restored hotel and B & B in two old Fort Seward officers' quarters. Restaurant and bar. *60 rooms, P.O. Box 1589, Tel. 766 20 00, Fax 766 24 45, Category 2*

SPORTS & LEISURE

Chilkat Guides
Guided rubber-dinghy tours on the Chilkat River through the American bald-eagle habitat. Also rafting expeditions lasting several days. *P.O. Box 170, Haines, AK 99827, Tel. 766 24 91, Fax 766 24 09*

Chilkat State Park
The peninsula in this nature reserve is a great place to spend a day hiking through ☙ magnificent fjord scenery. *South of Haines on Mud Bay Rd.*

Sockeye Cycle
Mountain bikes and kayak hire. Several days of touring into the Canadian Yukon Territory. *P.O. Box 829, Haines, AK 99827, Tel. and Fax 766 28 69*

INFORMATION

Haines Visitors' Bureau
Info centre in 2nd St. Postal address: P.O. Box 530, Haines, AK 99827, Tel. 766 22 34, Fax 766 31 55

JUNEAU

☛ **City Map inside back cover**

(108/C3) A US state capital with no road links to the outside world, no highways and no famous monuments. That's Alaska for you. Juneau (pop. 30,000), founded in 1880 on the occasion of a small gold strike, is certainly the US state capital with the most beautiful natural setting: nestled at the foot of steep Mt. Juneau with the dark waters of Gastineau Channel spread out before it. The city has splurged on only one big, showy government building, the *State Office Building* on Willoughby Ave. – the 8th-floor roof terrace affords a grand panoramic ☙ view out across the city.

A motley collection of Victorian houses and modern utilitarian buildings enlivens the downtown area around quirky Franklin St. This is where the cruise ships dock in summer. From here a *gondola-car lift* runs up the mountain. For evening fun, look in at the *Red Dog Saloon* and the historic ★ *bar of the Alaskan Hotel*, which can be quite lively. Take a stroll down the side-streets: at the corner of Gold and 5th streets the Russian Orthodox *St. Nicholas Church* (1894) and on 7th St. the meticulously restored *residence of Judge Wickersham* are both well worth visiting.

SIGHTS

Gastineau Salmon Hatchery
★ The underwater realm of the northern Pacific and salmon migrations are explained in the hatchery aquarium. *26197 Channel Drive, Mon–Fri 10 am–6 pm, Sat, Sun 12–5 pm, admission $3*

Mendenhall Glacier
The Juneau landmark: about 20 km north of the city, the broad glacier flows into a little lake. Visitor Centre, hiking trails. *Daily 8.30 am–5.30 pm, accessible to the public*

MUSEUM

Alaska State Museum

One of the best museums: exhibitions on the culture of the indigenous peoples and pioneer history. *395 Whittier St., daily 9 am–6 pm, admission $ 4*

RESTAURANTS

The Fiddlehead

An 'in' place; imaginative West Coast cuisine. Excellent seafood. *429 W Willoughby Ave., Tel. 586 31 50, Category 2*

Gold Creek Salmon Bake

A salmon picnic with a Gold Rush feeling. Fairly touristy, but the salmon tastes delicious. *1061 Salmon Lane, Tel. 789 00 52, Category 2*

SHOPPING

Franklin St. in the old town is lined with art galleries. Why not have a look at the *Rainsong Gallery (291 S Franklin St.),* or *Annie Kaill's (244 Front St.)* or *Raven's Journey (175 S Franklin St.)?*

ACCOMMODATION

Driftwood Lodge

Comfortable family hotel, downtown location. *62 rooms, 435 Willoughby Ave., Tel. 586 22 80, Fax 586 10 34, Category 2*

Mt. Juneau Inn

Friendly inn on the northern outskirts of town. *7 rooms, 1801 Old Glacier Hwy., Tel. 463 58 55, Fax 463 54 23, Category 2*

Silverbow Inn

Historic, beautifully restored downtown hotel. Very good restaurant.

10 rooms, 120 2nd St., Tel. 586 41 46, Fax 586 42 42, Category 1–2

Thayer Lake Lodge

A rustic wilderness lodge on remote Admiralty Island. *5 rooms, P.O. Box 5416, Ketchikan, AK 99901, Tel. 225 33 43, Fax 247 70 53, incl. three meals, Category 2*

SPORTS & LEISURE

Alaska Coastal Airlines

An air-taxi company that operates flightseeing, fishing and wilderness treks. Also trips to watch the bears on Pack Creek. *1873 Shell Simmons Drive, Juneau, AK 99801, Tel. 789 78 18*

Alaska Discovery Expeditions

★ Long camping trips in all regions of Alaska. Kayaking in Glacier Bay and around Admiralty Island. Rafting in the Arctic and white-water rafting down rivers. *5449-4D Shaune Drive, Juneau, AK 99801, Tel. 780 62 26, Fax 780 42 20*

Tracy Arm Tours

Day trips in boats to the icebergs and glaciers of Tracy Arm, a fjord to the south of Juneau. *2 Marine Way, Tel. 586 33 11*

INFORMATION

Juneau Visitors' Bureau

134 3rd St., Juneau, AK 99801, Tel. 586 22 01, Fax 586 63 04

SURROUNDING AREA

Admiralty Island/
Pack Creek   (108/C3–4)

The third biggest island in Southeast Alaska, Admiralty Island is almost entirely a nature reserve:

400,000 ha of unspoilt wilderness. Grizzly bears and eagles abound and salmon spawn in the island's many streams from July to September. One canoe route will take you right across the island. You can also explore the inlets along the coast by kayak. The mouth of Pack Creek is the perfect place for watching the grizzlies at your leisure (but permit required!). *Info: Forest Service, 101 Egan Drive, Juneau, AK 99801, Tel. 586 87 51, Fax 586 79 28*

KETCHIKAN

(**109/D5**) Ketchikan on the west coast of Revillagigedo Island is the first Alaskan port ferries and cruise ships reach if they are coming from the south. A typical Panhandle town, it boasts a busy fishing port framed by dark green mountains. Front St. is just as bustling as the port, with a host of saloons, art galleries and souvenir shops. Side-streets follow the coast and there's even a stream with leaping salmon. The town is small and quaint.

Ketchikan (pop. 15,000) is the second biggest city in Southeast Alaska after Juneau. Logging, tourism in recent years and, above all, the fisheries are the main sources of revenue. It is not just an idle boast when natives of Ketchikan style the city 'the capital of salmon fishing'. It is often given another, perhaps more dubious accolade. Ketchikan is Alaska's rain capital, with a record-breaking mean annual

Just like the olden days: Creek Street in Ketchikan

Totem Bight Park: art carved from wood

SIGHTS

Totem Heritage Center

Some 30 ancient totem poles from abandoned Southeast villages have been assembled here. A nature trail leads visitors through the little museum park. Across the stream a hatchery is informative on the life cycle of the salmon. *601 Deermount St., daily 8 am–5 pm, Sun from 9 am, admission $4*

Totem poles

The art legacy of the Tlingit Indians has been preserved in an exemplary way in Ketchikan. Several modern totem poles stand near the harbour. You can admire beautiful ancient carvings in *Saxman Park* (4 km south of town, with a wood-carving school and a gallery). The best place to become attuned to Native American culture is ★ *Totem Bight Historical Park* (15 km to the north on Tongass Hwy.), where a tribal clan house and 15 brightly painted historic poles are framed by the coastal forest.

precipitation of 4,000 mm. The thick northern rainforest around it and the moss growing on roofs attest to the abundant rain.

Downtown Front St. and Mill St. are thronged with visitors in summer when the cruise ships disgorge their passengers for some sightseeing. Despite this fact you can savour the charm of this historic town along Creek and Thomas streets, which are built out over the water on pilings. Until about 40 years ago, the red-light district of the fishing village was on Creek Street, where *Dolly's House (open by appointment)* is a light-hearted brothel museum. For a more serious look at the city's history, cross the stream and visit the *Tongass Historical Mu-*

RESTAURANTS

Cape Fox Lodge

Elegant restaurant with a view from a hill above the city centre – it even has a cog railway. *800 Venetia Way, Tel. 225 80 01, Fax 225 82 86, Category 1–2*

Waterfront Cafe

Coffee shop with a patio overlooking the water. Fresh seafood and hearty Alaska fare. *1287 Tongass Ave., Tel. 247 06 95, Category 3*

ACCOMMODATION

Best Western Landing
Pleasant hotel near the ferry dock at the northern end of Ketchikan. *76 rooms, 3434 Tongass Ave., Tel. 225 51 66, Fax 225 69 00, Category 2*

New York Hotel
Nicely restored historic hotel with a good restaurant. *8 rooms, 207 Stedman St., Tel. 225 02 46, Category 2*

Waterfall Resort
Fishing lodge in a converted old canning factory. Remote and quiet on Prince of Wales Island. *40 rooms, P.O. Box 6440, Ketchikan, AK 99901, Tel. 225 94 61, Fax 225 85 30, Category 1*

Yes Bay Lodge
A wilderness lodge in a perfect setting for fishing (salmon!) and enjoying the natural environment. Arrive from Ketchikan by floatplane. *12 rooms, postal address: P.O. Box 8660, Ketchikan, AK 99901, Tel. 800/999 07 84, Fax 907/225 85 30, incl. three meals, Category 1*

SPORTS & LEISURE

Southeast Exposure
Kayak hire and, most importantly, guided tours through ★ Misty Fjords National Monument. *P.O. Box 9143, Ketchikan, AK 99901, Tel. 225 88 29, Fax 225 88 49*

ENTERTAINMENT

The Ketchikan harbour bars can be pretty rough in the small hours, but this is the real Alaska.

Try the ❖ *Pioneer Bar (Front St./Mission St.)* or the ✝ *Potlatch Bar (Thomas St.).* Live music frequently in both.

INFORMATION

Ketchikan Visitors' Bureau
131 Front St., Ketchikan, AK 99901, Tel. 225 61 66, Fax 225 42 50

Southeast Alaska Visitor Center
Information on all regional nature reserves, exhibitions. Book wilderness cabin accommodation here. *50 Main St., Ketchikan, AK 99901, Tel. 228 62 14, Fax 228 26 34*

SURROUNDING AREA

Hyder (109/E5)
A gold-prospecting town (pop. 85) straight out of Jack London: façades leaning rakishly into the wind, dust blowing down Main St. and some shabby bars, the whole scene set in glacier-covered mountains. With neighbouring Stewart in Canada, Hyder is at the end of the *Portland Canal*, a fjord 145 km long. A ferry plies between Hyder and Ketchikan once a week. On *Fish Creek* near Hyder you can watch king salmon spawn in August. With any luck, you'll also spot bald eagles and brown bears. The dirt road along Fish Creek goes up into the *Coast Mountains* with scenic ✲ lookout points above Salmon Glacier, which stretches for 70 km.

Misty Fjords
National Monument (109/E5-6)
★ Undeveloped for tourism, the nature preserve (9,000 km²) is spectacular fjord country with

cliffs 1,000 m high, gem-like mountain lakes and high waterfalls. *Sightseeing tours from Ketchikan with Alaska Cruises (Tel. 225 60 44) or Taquan Air (Tel. 225 88 00)*

PETERSBURG

(**109/D4**) This town (pop. 3,500) on Mitkof Island thrives due to its salmon fisheries, as the presence of numerous *canning factories (daily guided tours)* on the long harbour front indicates. The name might make you think that this was originally a Russian town but you'd be wrong. In fact it was founded as a Norwegian settlement with one Peter Buschmann as its mayor in 1897. The town's inhabitants are proud of its Scandinavian background. Some of the houses – especially on lovely *Hammer Slough* – still boast *rosmaling*, typical Norwegian vernacular

painting, and in front of the *Sons of Norway Hall* stands the model of a doughty Viking ship. Just south of town the ferry negotiates an extremely tight passage called the *Wrangell Narrows*, a spectacular section of the beautiful Inside Passage.

SPORTS & LEISURE

Tongass Kayak Adventures
Kayaks for hire and guided day tours. Longer trips in the Stikine delta. *P.O. Box 2169, Tel. 772 46 00, Fax 772 39 40*

Viking Travel
Reservations for whale-watching trips, charter fishing boats and trips to *Le Conte Glacier*, Alaska's southernmost glacier, which flows into the sea. *On the harbour, 101 N Nordic Drive, Tel. 772 38 18, Fax 772 39 40*

All the crab you can eat: Petersburg lives on the sea's bounty

Your best bet: wilderness cabins

Alaska isn't cheap, granted, but still there are ways and means of making your dream of a wilderness holiday in a lonely cabin by a lake come true and at a price you can afford. Scattered far and wide across the National Forests and national parks are about 250 Public Recreation Cabins. These are simply rough log cabins which sleep up to six people. The price is only $10–25 a night – for the whole cabin! You'll be self-catering: that means you have to bring your own sleeping bag, cooker and provisions. Most cabins do have a canoe or rowing boat. However, to reach your dream cabin, you'll probably have to foot the bill for a charter flight (about $150–300). Many cabins are right on hiking trails. You can book cabins with the Public Lands Information Centers (PLICs) up to six months in advance. The PLICs will send you a list of cabins available. Even if you haven't booked in advance, it's worth inquiring at a Forest Service bureau or at the nearest PLIC anyway. There's sure to be an unoccupied log cabin out there somewhere.

ACCOMMODATION

Tides Inn

Good motel at the centre of town. Some rooms with kitchenettes. Bicycle hire. *46 rooms, 1st St./Dolphin St., Tel. 772 42 88, Fax 772 42 86, Category 2*

INFORMATION

Petersburg Visitor's Center

Information office, 1st St./Fram St., P.O. Box 649, Petersburg, AK 99833, Tel. 772 46 36, Fax 772 36 46

SITKA

(**108/B4**) Here you feel close to Russia. Once the capital of Russian Alaska, Sitka (pop. 9,200) on the west coast of Baranof Island has become thoroughly Americanized but it still likes to look back to the days when it was an outpost of tsarist Russia. Shops are full of babushka dolls, the New Archangel Dancers folklore group performs Russian dances and the Orthodox priest in meticulously restored *St. Michael's Cathedral* is proud of the original Russian icons in his care.

From ⬧ *Castle Hill*, where Governor Baranof built his residence in 1804 to mark the founding of the colony, you have a superb view across the city, the islands off shore and Sitka's very own volcano, *Mt. Edgecomb.* Castle Hill is where the purchase of Alaska was officially recorded in 1867 and the American flag was first flown in Alaska. In the *Centennial Building* on the harbour you can visit the little *Isabel Miller Museum (in summer daily 9 am–5 pm)* to look at a model of the city as it was in those days.

SIGHTS

Alaska Raptor Rehabilitation Center

A 'nursing home' for ailing bald eagles and other raptors: the perfect opportunity to see one of these magnificent birds close up. *1101 Sawmill Creek Rd., in summer daily 9 am–4 pm, admission $6*

Sitka National Historical Park
Handsomely painted totem poles and commemorative panels in the ❄ park remind you that the Tlingit settlement here was destroyed by the Russians in 1804. Abutting the Visitor Center is a *wood-carving workshop*, where you can watch Native American artists at work. *At the east end of Lincoln St., daily 8 am–5 pm, admission free*

MUSEUMS

Russian Bishop's House
The carefully restored Orthodox bishop's residence gives a good idea of what life was like under the Russian colonial administration in 1842. *Lincoln St., in summer daily 9 am–1 pm and 2 pm–5 pm, admission $3*

Sheldon Jackson Museum
★ Outstanding ethnographic exhibitions dealing with the indigenous peoples of Alaska: Tlingit wood carvings, Aleut kayaks and Inuit masks. The museum is on the campus of a college that is also called Sheldon Jackson and is Alaska's oldest school. *104 College Drive, in summer daily 9 am–5 pm, admission $3*

ACCOMMODATION

Alaska Ocean View B & B
Quiet little B & B with a ❄ view of the bay. Lots of tours on offer. *3 rooms, 1101 Edgecumbe Drive, Tel. 747 83 10, Fax 747 34 40, Category 2*

Westmark Shee Atika
Modern, first-class hotel at centre of town. Tastefully decorated with Native American art. Nice restaurant and bar. *101 rooms, 330 Seward St., Tel. 747 62 41, Fax 747 54 86, Category 1*

SPORTS & LEISURE

Baidarka Boats
Kayak hire and guided day trips by kayak through the fjords around Sitka. *201 Lincoln St., Sitka, AK 99835, Tel. 747 89 96*

Sitka's Secrets
Boat trips in small groups to watch otters, whales, seabirds and eagles. *500 Lincoln St., Tel. 747 50 89*

INFORMATION

Sitka Visitors' Bureau
Info office in the Centennial Building on the harbour, P.O. Box 1226, Sitka, AK 99835, Tel. 747 59 40, Fax 747 37 39

SKAGWAY

(108/B1) A century ago, gold prospectors thronged Skagway, the northernmost Inside Passage port and gateway to the Yukon. It often had an itinerant population of over 20,000 then. However, the adventurers didn't linger long because they had to make it across forbidding Chilkoot Pass before frost set in and to continue on down the Yukon River to the Klondike goldfields. Skagway must have been wild in those days: a jumble of general stores and dingy saloons, back-country brothels and stalls for horses. Soapy Smith and his notorious gang of outlaws robbed greenhorns of all their money and shoot-outs were the order of the day. A railway line was built in 1900 from Skagway harbour at the end of the Lynn Canal to Whitehorse in the Canadian Yukon Territory.

The Gold Rush boom was over in only three years. Skagway survived as a sleepy station for goods trains transporting ore. In 1981 a road was built across White Pass into the Canadian Yukon Territory so that it is now easy to retrace by car the gold prospectors' arduous trek into the interior.

Today about 800 people live in the tiny town nestled cosily in the mountains. A new boom era has dawned: tourism. Nostalgia reigns, as a cluster of restored buildings on Broadway, Skagway's high street, clearly shows. Of course they don't house brothels nowadays; they're bursting with souvenir shops. Every day in summer big cruise ships dock in the port, releasing hordes of day trippers into the town. For all the hustle and hype, it's still worth sauntering through the Gold Rush sites. You can visit the *Historic District* with many buildings dating from 1899 to 1910 or *Bernard Moore House* featuring exhibits and furnishings depicting family life at that time. You'll find a good Walking Tour Map in the Visitors' bureau on Broadway. All the historic buildings are marked on it – even the gold prospectors' cemetery, where the local outlaw hero, Soapy Smith, is buried. He died as he had lived, shot down by a vengeful bullet.

MUSEUMS

Klondike Gold Rush National Historical Park

Excellent exhibitions dealing with the Gold Rush era in the old train station. Offering films and guided tours. *Broadway/2nd Ave., in summer daily 6 am–7 pm, other seasons 9 am–6 pm, admission free*

Trail of '98 Museum

A delightful collection of relics from gold hunters. Exhibiting fine historic photos. *On the upper floor of the Town Hall in 7th Ave, in summer daily 9 am–5 pm, admission $2*

RESTAURANT

Historic Skagway Inn

A stylish evening restaurant in what was once – in 1897 – a brothel. Part of it is a B & B inn. *12 rooms, 7th Ave./Broadway, Tel. 983 22 89, Fax 983 27 13, Category 2*

SHOPPING

Whether you're looking for a T-shirt or a gold nugget, it will be entirely your own fault if you don't find it in the shops on Broadway. Sifting through all the kitsch can be daunting, but you should take a look at the exhibitions of *walrus ivory scrimshaw* at *Corrington's (Broadway/5th Ave.)* as well as the *moccasins* and *reindeer leather gloves* in the *Made in Skagway Gallery*.

ACCOMMODATION

Golden North Hotel

Alaska's oldest hotel. Not terribly modern, but lots of ambience in the evenings. *31 rooms, Broadway/3rd Ave., Tel. 983 24 51, Fax 983 27 55, Category 2*

Gold Rush ambience on Broadway in Skagway

Wind Valley Lodge
A modern motel on the northern outskirts of town. Restaurant. *29 rooms, 22nd St./State St., Tel. 983 22 36, Fax 983 29 57, Category 2*

SPORTS & LEISURE

Chilkoot Trail
★ This is the legendary trail taken by the gold prospectors at Dyea, a derelict mining camp near Skagway. It crosses the Chilkoot Pass at 1,067 m and goes on to Bennet in the Canadian Yukon Territory. A highly popular tour among hikers, who love the beautiful scenery. It takes about four days and covers 53 km. *Information on the trail and the necessary permits in advance from: Klondike Gold Rush National Historical Park, P.O. Box 517, Skagway, AK 99840, Tel. 983 29 21, Fax 983 20 46*

ENTERTAINMENT

Red Onion Saloon
An institution, with a fabulous old bar and live music. The locals come in the evening. *Broadway/2nd Ave.*

INFORMATION

Skagway Visitors' Bureau
Broadway, P.O. Box 1025, Skagway, AK 99840, Tel. 983 28 54, Fax 983 38 54

SURROUNDING AREA

White Pass & Yukon Route (104/C5–6)
A real treat for railway buffs: the historic narrow-gauge railway huffs and puffs as it did in 1900 up the ↘ White Pass into Canadian Yukon Territory. Shuttle bus to Whitehorse. *P.O. Box 435, Tel. 983 22 17, Fax 983 27 34*

WRANGELL

(**109/D4**) A fishing village and trading post (pop. 2,400) founded in 1834 by the Russians, Wrangell seems to have been almost overlooked by tourism. It is nestled in green mountains and magnificent fjords near the mouth of the mighty Stikine River. Only the little ❦ harbour is a hive of activity almost all day long. From here the *excursion boats* leave for the broad river delta, where you can watch moose, seals and eagles to your heart's content.

In town the *Wrangell Museum (open by appointment)* is astonishingly informative on the history of the region. Another absolute must is *Chief Shakes Island*, a little island in the harbour on which a full-scale reconstruction of a typical, lavishly decorated Tlingit clan house has been built. Walking up and down *Petroglyph Beach*, you will discover a great many ancient petroglyphs, drawings incised on the dark rock. On the *boardwalk* local children sell garnet crystals which can be found in this region.

ACCOMMODATION

Roadhouse Lodge
A rustic lodge outside town which operates fishing charter boats as well as rafting and jet-boarding. Boats can be chartered for salmon fishing and canoeing on the Stikine River. *10 rooms, P. O. Box 1199, Tel. 874 23 35, Fax 874 31 04, Category 3*

Stikine Inn
An unpretentious hotel with a ❦ harbour view. Restaurant and ❦ bar. *34 rooms, P.O. Box 990, Tel. 874 33 88, Fax 874 39 23, Category 2*

INFORMATION

Wrangell Visitor Center
P.O. Box 49, Wrangell, AK 99929, Tel. 874 39 01, Fax 874 39 05

SURROUNDING AREA

Anan Creek   (**109/D5**)
From mid-July to September, grizzlies and brown bears gather along this creek to fish for salmon (guided bear-watching tours from Wrangell and Ketchikan). *About 60 km south of Wrangell*

The bald eagle: the US emblem

Alaska is the last stronghold of the American bald eagle: about 40,000 of them live on its coasts and lakes. The largest raptors in North America, these awe-inspiring birds have a wingspan of more than 2 m. They can live up to 40 years and are monogamous. Their heads don't turn white until they have reached maturity at the age of five. They love to feast on salmon, which is why the world's biggest congregation of bald eagles, comprising up to 4,000 members, convenes in the bare trees along the Chilkat River near Haines. There they stay from late October to January, a thrilling sight for ornithologists and photographers.

Where all roads end

Wild country, lonely tundra and gale-battered islands – trips that call for careful planning

Alaskans call the unpopulated interior and back country of their vast state simply *the bush.* This means all towns, islands and regions inaccessible by road. The term covers most of Alaska. The Alaskan bush in fact stretches from the Aleutian Islands strung across the northern Pacific to the vast marshes and lakes in the Yukon delta, the stony coasts of the Bering Strait, the peaks of the Brooks Range and all the way north to the tundra bordering the Arctic Ocean.

Wilderness everywhere. Man has had very little chance to impair the ecological balance here. Fortunately, most Alaskan ecosystems are protected by law nowadays. Caribou herds hundreds of thousands strong roam the valleys of Kobuk Valley National Park. Millions of waterfowl migrate every summer to the Yukon delta to nest and hatch their young. Huge brown bears jostle each other on

July is fishing season for bears: brown bears catching salmon at the Katmai National Park waterfalls

the banks of salmon streams in Katmai National Park and Kodiak Island to land the fish leaping up the rapids to spawn, ignoring the crowds of curious human onlookers who have intruded on their territory to stare at them.

Its raging rivers, snow-capped peaks and icy coasts make the Alaskan bush one of the world's last paradises, a place where nature-lovers, bird-watchers and eco-freaks can be at one with nature. One thing to remember though, is that it's difficult, and expensive, to go to Alaska just to see the sights. Some regions can be visited only on guided tours, not just because it would be dangerous to do anything else, but also because the unspoilt natural beauty of these regions is less infringed on by such tours than by individual incursions. Then there are regions where you can venture off on your own, provided you've planned your trip carefully, are properly equipped and are in prime physical condition. Watch out for the short (and expensive) trips that are so often advertised. A three-day

MARCO POLO SELECTION: THE BUSH

1 Board of Trade Saloon
The wildest bar this
side of Sibiria: manners
are as rough and ready
as the lifestyle here
(page 77)

2 Kodiak bears
Bears and salmon:
fun to watch them both
in action (page 76)

3 The Pribilof Islands
Visit fur seals and
several seabird colonies
(page 77)

**4 Valley of
Ten Thousand Smokes**
A volcanic landscape
formed of ash – with
bears to boot
(page 76)

trip to the Pribilof Islands or to see the bears in Katmai or on Kodiak Island is an unforgettable experience. By contrast, a day trip to, for example, Barrow, to desolate Inuit settlements, is pure mass tourism. Only if you stayed there for several days, you might develop some insight into the people and their problems. Cultural decline and social disorientation have devastated the indigenous peoples of this beautiful country.

ALEUTIAN ISLANDS

(**O**) The volcanic Aleutian chain is a 1,600-km-long arc almost reaching Sibiria. Rain, fog and gales make life on these 200 islands separating the Pacific from the Bering Sea almost unendurable. These days, only four islands are inhabited, since the Russians deported many indigenous Aleuts and then the US Army moved most of the rest when the Japanese occupied two of the islands during World War II. *Unalaska/Dutch Harbor* is now the largest settlement (pop. 3,000 in summer) and the most

important fishing port on the Bering Sea, which still teems with fish. Almost the entire chain of islands is now a *bird sanctuary* – and it's very difficult to travel about here at the best of times. A few expedition cruise ships come in summer. Once a month a ship from the Alaska Marine Highway fleet plies between Homer and Dutch Harbor.

BARROW

(**O**) You should come up here only if you're absolutely dying to stick your finger in the Arctic Ocean. The flight to Alaska's northernmost town (pop. 4,000), 500 km north of the Arctic Circle, is long and exhausting. The local Inupiat Eskimo tribe has become fairly affluent owing to the oil strikes on Prudhoe Bay to the east (the central processing plant may be visited only by guided tours) but the place still looks rather bleak and desolate even though a number of modern buildings has sprung up. This is truly the end of the world.

GATES OF THE ARCTIC NATIONAL PARK

(**O**) Uncharted mountain fastnesses, 34,000 km² of wilderness, no roads, let alone hiking trails – the biggest national park in northern Alaska incorporates much of the Brooks Range (2,600 m). During the summer, which is unfortunately very brief, the tundra is carpeted with wild flowers. In autumn, caribou migrate south through the valleys before winter returns for eight months to blanket the region with ice. Trips start at the tiny settlements of *Bettles* and *Anaktuvuk Pass.* Two adventure activities you can engage in here are *canoeing and rafting* on such rivers as the Alatna, the Koyukuk and the Noatak.

Sourdough Outfitters
Guided hiking and rafting expeditions in the park and other northern wilderness regions. Also rental equipment and organized tours. *P.O. Box 26066, Bettles, AK 99726, Tel. 692 52 52, Fax 692 55 57*

Gates of the Arctic National Park
P.O. Box 74680, Fairbanks, AK 99707, Tel. 456 02 81, Fax 456 04 52

KATMAI NATIONAL PARK

(**107/D-E2-3**) Covering 16,000 km², this vast nature reserve on the

Ashes to ashes: the Valley of Ten Thousand Smokes

Alaska Peninsula was created by a horrendous volcanic eruption in 1912, when a layer of volcanic ash 200 m thick covered the entire region north of Novarupta Crater. Sulphurous steam issued from it for years afterwards. This is the spectacular ★ *Valley of Ten Thousand Smokes* (guided tours by bus and good hiking trails). In addition, the park is famous for *brown bears*, which congregate in droves along the coast and the Brooks River to fish for salmon. From the ◁☝▷ *observation platform at Brooks Falls* you can watch these tough, shaggy customers at work, catching all the salmon they can eat. But you'll have to book well in advance for rooms in *Brooks Lodge (16 rooms, incl. three meals, Category 1)* near the falls (the best way to do it is through your travel agent). There are also day trips leaving from Anchorage if the lodge is booked up.

Katmai National Park
P.O. Box 7, King Salmon, AK 99613, Tel. 246 33 05, Fax 246 42 86

KODIAK ISLAND

(107/E–F3–4) A single road leads to the thickly forested northern region of Alaska's biggest island. It encircles the island capital, Kodiak (pop. 6,500), a bustling port town founded in 1784 by the Russians. The rest of this big, mountainous island (9,300 km²) is a wilderness nature reserve with vast stretches of tundra in the south and long rocky beaches. It is the habitat of about 3,000 brown bears, the celebrated *Kodiak bears.* They are the world's biggest grizzlies, weighing in at up to 700 kg. A number of little charter companies operate ★ *bearwatching tours* when the Kodiak bears, like most other Alaskan bears, gather at the salmon rivers in summer to eat their fill: *for instance Uyak Air (Tel. 486 34 07) or Sea Hawk Air (Tel. 486 82 82).*

In Kodiak you can visit the *Baranof Museum (in summer daily 10 am–4 pm)* in an old fur cold-storage house to learn about the island's Russian colonial past. The *Alutiq Center (open by appointment)* exhibits kayaks and wares woven by the indigenous Aleuts. In Fort Abercrombie State Park there is a beautiful camping site. Scenic footpaths follow the coast. If you want to go *salmon fishing*, you can stay at one of the pleasant lodges in the interior.

Kodiak Island Visitors' Bureau
100 Marine Way, Kodiak, AK 99615, Tel. 486 47 82, Fax 486 65 45

KOTZEBUE

(O) An ancient Inupiat settlement on a low-lying peninsula jutting into the Bering Strait, Kotzebue lies right on the Arctic Circle. In 1816, Otto von Kotzebue, a German seafarer and explorer in the service of the Russians, discovered the settlement, which was later named after him. About 3,000 people live here, mainly due to hunting and fishing. Nowadays Kotzebue has modern amenities, such as prefabricated houses and snowmobiles. This is the starting-off point for *kayak trips* along the coast of the Bering

Strait and *wilderness tours* into the remote fastnessses of Kobuk Valley National Park as well as *rafting expeditions* on the Noatak River.

MUSEUM

Nana Museum of the Arctic

Exhibition and cultural centre of the Inupiats, who also perform dances and give concerts of Eskimo songs. *Open for tours from May to September, admission $25*

NOME

(**O**) A medley of Western façades and prefabricated dwellings, where both Inupiat and Alaskans of European descent live, this rough, tough bush town (pop. 4,500) is by far the most interesting of its kind in the Arctic: 20,000 gold prospectors lived here in 1900. Gold was found in the black sand on the shores of Norton Sound. Even today the skeletons of derelict *dredges* and engines left over from mining bear silent witness to the boom era. The little *Carrie McLain Museum (in summer daily 9 am–6 pm)* housed in the town library shows what those wild days were like.

The gold prospectors also left a network of dirt tracks about 400 km long that will take you into ↘↙ the mountains and all through the tundra. Rent a car or hike to the *Inupiat village of Teller*, or lovely *Pilgrim Hot Springs*, an oasis of warm water in the wilderness or into the bush, where you might catch sight of musk-ox and reindeer. Or you can always grab a sieve and start panning for gold. People are still doing it on the beach and some of them strike gold.

ACCOMMODATION

Nugget Inn

A clean rustic hotel right on the waterfront. Restaurant. *47 rooms, Front St., Tel. 443 23 23, Fax 443 59 66, Category 2*

ENTERTAINMENT

There's always been nightlife in Nome – but it can be pretty rough. Why not try the ★ *Board of Trade Saloon* on Front St.?

INFORMATION

Nome Visitors' Bureau

P.O. Box 240, Nome, AK 99762, Tel. 443 55 35, Fax 443 58 32

PRIBILOF ISLANDS

(**O**) ★ St. George and St. Paul, two tiny isolated islands in the Bering Sea, are a fabulous Garden of Eden for animals – a Galapagos of the far north. Gabriel Pribilof, a Russian fur trader, discovered the islands in 1768. Fur seals in their hundreds of thousands congregate in July on the pebble beaches of the island to bear their young. Observant bird-watchers can see colonies of more than two million seabirds on the steep cliffs: guillemots, auks and at least 200 more species.

Camping is prohibited here. The only possibility of visiting islands inhabited by Aleut fishermen is to sign up for one of the guided tours operated by several companies. They last several days and you stay at St. Paul's only hotel.

In Jack London's footsteps

The call of the wild will lure you like the gold prospectors of yore to the Yukon Territory

For romantic adventurers, the Yukon (officially this is the Yukon Territory) on the northwestern tip of Canada is the one place to go in the far north. This is where the biggest Gold Rush of all time took place. Towns like Dawson City and the Klondike region were once famous throughout the world. In the early years of the present century, adventurers poured into the Yukon from the four corners of the earth to try their luck in the gold-fields of the far north. No hardship could deter them. The hope of instant riches kept them going through the trackless wilderness. The Gold Rush lasted only a few years. Jack London wrote stories and novels about it. Robert Service, the 'Bard of the Klondike', wrote ballads and poems, collected as 'Songs of a Sourdough'. Charlie Chaplin's film *Gold Rush* is a classic.

You can still find lots of gold-prospecting nostalgia in the Yukon. However, more importantly, there's still a lot of wilderness and superb scenery to explore there.

Still prospecting

In the south, the St. Elias Mountains boast Canada's highest peak, Mt. Logan (5,959 m). This mighty barrier shields the interior from Pacific clouds heavy with rain, thus regulating precipitation and ensuring days of sun all year. In the far north the tundra is interspersed with lower mountain ranges. Huge herds of caribou roam through the valleys here as they have done since prehistoric times.

The only part of the Yukon (483,000 km^2) to have been developed at all is the south. Two-thirds of its population of roughly 31,000 live in the Territory's only city, Whitehorse, the capital of the Yukon. About 6,000 Dena Indians live in the Yukon, in settlements scattered throughout the interior. In recent years they have been able to lay claim to their own land after lengthy negotiations with the Canadian government.

The most important traffic artery through the Yukon is still the Alaska Highway. Now paved for its full length, it was built in just eight months in 1942 during World War II by the US Army in collaboration with Canada.

Branching off it into the interior are side-roads, such as Canol Road, which runs up into the wilderness region of the Mackenzie Mountains, and the Klondike Highway to the historic gold-fields where Jack London prospected near Dawson City and on south to the Alaskan port of Skagway.

However, you don't have to stick to the highways. Why not take a leisurely canoeing or kayak trip on the Yukon River from Whitehorse to Dawson City? You can always follow in the footsteps of the gold prospectors by hiking across the Chilkoot Pass. White-water rafting in Kluane National Park is yet another way of exploring the beautiful Yukon.

ATLIN, B.C.

(108/C1) ★ Remarkable for its beautiful ☟ setting on a lake of the same name, Atlin is worth a detour of about 100 km from the Alaska Highway. A weather-beaten gold prospectors' settlement founded in 1898 during the great Klondike Gold Rush, Atlin is actually in British Columbia although it is only accessible from the Yukon. Nowadays only 400 people live in and around Atlin, most of them gold prospectors, artists and drop-outs. Here you shouldn't miss taking a flight over the glacier-covered Coast Mountains. For this spectacular undertaking *try Summit Air Charter, Tel. 250/ 651 76 00.*

ACCOMMODATION

Noland House
A stylishly restored house converted into a very attractive B & B inn. *4 rooms, P.O. Box 135, Atlin, Tel. and Fax 250/651 75 85, Category 2*

DAWSON CITY

(104/B2) The Gold Rush era is still with us in this almost-ghost town (pop. 2,000) that was once celebrated as the 'Paris of the North'. During the Klondike Gold Rush in 1900 it had a population of 30,000: adventurers, dance-hall girls, mining engineers and saloon

MARCO POLO SELECTION: THE YUKON AND THE ALASKA HIGHWAY

1 Atlin, B.C.
Spectacular mountain scenery and Gold Rush ambience (page 80)

2 Dempster Highway
A road through 700 km of wilderness from Dawson City to the Mackenzie delta (page 82)

3 SS Klondike
The Grand Old Lady of Yukon ships (page 85)

4 White-water rafting in Kluane National Park
The Tatshenshini River is the grandest white-water river in the North (pages 83 and 86)

Dawson City: Diamond Tooth Gertie and the Can-Can Girls

proprietors. Plank sidewalks and weathered clapboard façades in the Wild West style make Dawson look like a film set. In *Diamond Tooth Gertie's Gambling Hall* you can see Can-Can Girls dance. At the *Palace Grand Theatre* melodramas put you in the mood and in what is said to have been *Jack London's cabin* a Jack London lookalike gives readings from his novels.

Many of the restored old buildings are open to the public, such as the *Post Office* in King Street, *Harrington's Store* on *3rd Ave. (photo exhibition)* and the historic *paddlewheel steamer 'SS Keno'* moored by the banks of the Yukon River. For the loveliest 🔆 view of town, climb the oddly named *Midnight Dome*, a hill with a tortuous dirt track winding up it.

This town at the mouth of the Klondike River survives on Yukon tourism. All around it, however, unregenerate hopefuls are still prospecting for gold. On Saturday evenings the saloons are lively when the miners come into town to celebrate a week's gleanings with libations of Canadian and American whisky.

Dawson City Museum

Historic photos and all sorts of mining implements evoke the town's heyday. Daily film shows documenting Gold Rush history, slide shows and gold-prospecting equipment for panning gold. *5th Ave./Church St., in summer daily 10 am–6 pm, admission Can $4*

Robert Service Cabin

Klondike Bard's log cabin (1898) lovingly restored. At 10 am and

3 pm he comes to life to read his comical 'The Shooting of Dan McGrew', 'The Cremation of Sam McGee' and 'Ballads of a Cheechako'. *8th Ave./Mission St., in summer daily 9 am–5 pm, admission Can $6*

Klondike Kate's
A cosy old place to eat, with a patio; big menu. Serves good coffee. *3rd. Ave./King St., Tel. 867/993 65 27, Category 2*

Dawson City Bunkhouse
Simple rooms in a new house made to look historic. Showers in the hall. *16 rooms, Princess St., Bag 4040, Dawson City, Tel. 867/993 61 64, Fax 993 60 51, Category 2*

Eldorado
Has been the best address in Dawson for a long time, which isn't saying much. The 52 rooms are modern and comfortable but certainly not luxurious. Restaurant and saloon. *3rd Ave./Princess St., Tel. 867/993 54 51, Fax 993 52 56, Category 1*

Fifth Avenue B & B
A modern, sparkling clean inn close to the museum. *4 rooms, 5th Ave./Mission St., Tel. and Fax 867/ 993 59, Category 2*

Visitor Reception Centre
The visitors' centre puts on a slide show and hosts guided tours of town. *Front St./King St., Tel. 867/993 55 66, Fax 993 56 83*

Bonanza Creek (104/B2)
In August 1896 the first gold strike was made in this tributary valley of the Klondike River. Enormous ore tips and a huge gold ore-washing facility, *Dredge No. 4*, show how hard the gold prospectors had to work.

Top of the World Highway (104/A–B1–2)
The most scenic link between Alaska and the Yukon ☆ is a panoramic highway running for 270 km through remote mountain peaks, green valleys, goldfields and endless forests. There is only one 'town' along the way, an old mining camp called *Chicken* (pop. 37). Now open only in summer, the road is – unfortunately – due to be improved and paved.

DEMPSTER HIGHWAY

(104/B1–2) ★ Crossing the Arctic Circle, this road runs north through the wilderness for over 700 km from Dawson City through empty tundra regions to the Mackenzie delta. Along the way, the only signs of human habitation are tiny Native American settlements and a filling station. This is real Arctic scenery: first taiga, predominantly coniferous woodland, and then, in the Richardson Mountains further north, the tundra, which is carpeted in summer with wild flowers. The drive is particularly beautiful in early September when the foliage turns red and gold.

At the end of the road is *Inuvik* **(101/F3)**. The biggest town in the western Arctic region, it looks like something out of a Lego set. The houses are as brightly painted as Easter eggs. About 3,000 people live here: Inuit, Dena and other Alaskans, at the eastern edge of the vast Mackenzie delta. The name of the town means 'Place for Mankind', an apt designation.

There is a remarkable church here shaped like an igloo. Also recommended in the area: *flights above the surrounding countryside*: for example to *the trapper settlement of Aklavik* in the 80-km-wide river delta, to the old *whaling station on Herschel Island* or to the *Inuit settlement of Tuktoyaktuk* on the coast of the Arctic Ocean or to see the herds of Arctic musk-ox on *Banks Island* around the Inuit settlement of *Sachs Harbour*.

TOURS

Arctic Nature Tours
Flights into the Mackenzie delta, to Herschel Island and into all the huge national parks in the northern Yukon Territory. *P.O. Box 1530, Inuvik, Tel. 867/777 33 00, Fax 777 34 00*

ACCOMMODATION

Eagle Plains Hotel
The only beds available for 300 km around: a sparkling clean, friendly container hotel with a restaurant and a bar. *32 rooms, at km 371, Tel. and Fax 867/993 24 53, Category 2*

Mackenzie Hotel
A modern hotel in town centre with a restaurant and pub. *55 rooms, P.O. Box 1618, Inuvik, Tel. 867/777 28 61, Fax 777 33 17, Category 1–2*

KLUANE NATIONAL PARK/ HAINES JUNCTION

(**104/A–B4–5**) Encircled by mountains, tiny *Haines Junction* on the Alaska Highway is the point of departure for trips into *Kluane National Park* ($22,000$ km^2), an entirely undeveloped, unspoilt wilderness bordering Alaska. There, in the ice-clad St. Elias Mountains, the lofty peak of *Mt. Logan*, Canada's highest mountain, soars to 5,959 m. The Alaska Highway runs along the northern rim of the park to the shores of ↘ *Kluane Lake* (400 km^2 in area). A network of hiking trails ranging from easy to advanced covers the foothills of the Kluane Range. In the eastern part of the park, accessible from Haines Highway, you'll find camping sites and extensive trails at *Lake Kathleen*.

In the Park Visitor Center at Haines Junction, Rangers will provide you with tips for *hikes* and *rafting expeditions* on the glacier rivers. A really thrilling experience is a *flightseeing tour* of the glaciers: *Sifton Air, Tel. 867/634 29 16*.

SPORTS & LEISURE

Canadian River Expeditions
Six- to twelve-day rubber-dinghy expeditions on the ★ *Tatshenshini* and other northern rivers. *Postal address: P.O. Box 1023, Whistler, Canada, B.C. V0N 1B0, Tel. 604/938 66 51, Fax 938 66 21*

Kluane Adventure Centre
The place to book all local guided hiking tours, rides, mountain-

bike tours and round-trip flights. Also long rafting expeditions in the Park and on the ★ Tatshenshini River. *Haines Hwy., Tel. 867/634 23 13, Fax 634 28 02*

ACCOMMODATION

The Cabin B & B

A cluster of cosy log cabins on the eastern fringe of Kluane National Park. About 40 km south of Haines Junction. Just the place for starting out on hikes. *P.O. Box 5334, Haines Junction, Tel. and Fax 867/634 26 26, Category 3*

Cozy Corner

A good, unpretentious motel on the Alaska Highway; restaurant. *12 rooms, P.O. Box 5406, Haines Junction, Tel. 867/634 25 11, Fax 634 21 19, Category 2*

Dalton Trail Lodge

A Swiss-run lodge about 40 km south of town on the edge of Kluane National Park. Fishing, canoeing trips and riding. *15 rooms, P.O. Box 5331, Haines Junction, Tel. and Fax 867/667 10 99, Category 2*

INFORMATION

Kluane National Park

Visitor Centres in Haines Junction and at Sheep Mountain on the Alaska Highway. *Postal address: P.O. Box 5495, Haines Junction, Canada, YT Y0B 1L0, Tel. 867/634 72 07, Fax 634 72 08*

WATSON LAKE

(**105/F5**) Since the Alaska Highway was built in 1942, this town (pop. 1,800) in the southern Yukon Territory has been a major hub for supplies, provisioning the entire region. Another relic of that era is the *Watson Lake Signpost Forest*, a vast forest of road signs with place-names from all over the world, allegedly started by a homesick soldier stationed here. Next to the signpost forest, a modern *Interpretive Centre* tells the story of building the Alaska Highway.

SURROUNDING AREA

Nahanni National Park   (O)

A park for white-water rafters: the *South Nahanni River* flows for 320 km through the Mackenzie Mountains and plunges 90 m over lovely *Virginia Falls* to rage through gorges with walls up to 900 m high. *For guided trips, contact Nahanni River Adventures, P.O. Box 4869, Whitehorse, YT Canada, Y1A 4N6, Tel. 867/668 31 80, Fax 668 30 56*

WHITEHORSE

(**104/C5**) The bustling capital (pop. 23,000) of the Yukon Territory sprawls along the broad banks of the Yukon River. Supermarkets, motels, restaurants and modern buildings cluster around Main St.: civilization in the wilderness. It is of fairly recent date. A settlement sprang up here in 1898, when thousands of gold-seekers pushed through Miles Canyon above what is now the town on rafts and makeshift boats to reach the Klondike gold-fields. Whitehorse was not made the capital of the Yukon Territory until 1953, after the Alaska Highway was built. It is the place to stock up on all necessary supplies and staples. It also boasts some historic attractions. On the narrow-gauge *White Pass & Yukon Railway*, steam-engine driven trains take visitors on a delightfully scenic trip in summer from Whitehorse (shuttle bus to the train) through the Coast Mountains to the Gold Rush port of Skagway in Alaska, where the once notorious *Chilkoot Pass* begins.

Yukon river travel makes the 'good old days' come alive again. *2nd Ave./Yukon River, in summer daily 9 am–6 pm, guided tours, admission Can $3.75*

Yukon Transportation Museum

Snowshoes, dog sleds, old bush planes and jeeps to show how the far north was won. *Alaska Hwy., at the airport, in summer daily 10 am–6 pm, admission Can $3.50*

MUSEUMS

MacBride Museum

Historic photos and gold-prospecting equipment tell the stirring history of the town. *1st St./Wood St., in summer daily 10 am–6 pm, admission Can $4*

SS Klondike

★ Nostalgia plus: a splendidly restored paddle-wheel steamer dating from the heyday of

SHOPPING

Murdoch's

Gold-nugget jewellery. *207 Main St.*

Northern Images

Superb Inuit soapstone sculpture, art reproductions and fur-trimmed parkas handmade by the Inuit in tiny settlements on the Arctic Ocean. *311 Jarvis St.*

In dry dock: the paddle-wheel steamer 'SS Klondike' in Whitehorse

Kanoe People

Rental of canoes and canoeing equipment for expeditions on the Yukon River to Dawson City. *P.O. Box 5152, Whitehorse, Canada, YT Y1A 4S3, Tel. 867/668 48 99, Fax 668 48 91*

Sky High Wilderness Ranches

Day trips and longer excursions on horseback up into the Coast Mountains south of town. *P.O. Box 4482, Whitehorse, Canada, YT Y1A 2R8, Tel. 867/ 667 43 21, Fax 668 26 33*

Tatshenshini Expediting

Day trips and longer expeditions by rubber dinghy and canoe on the ★ Tatshenshini and other rivers. *1602 Alder St., Whitehorse, Canada, YT Y1A 3W8, Tel. 867/633 27 42, Fax 633 61 84*

Wanderlust Wilderness Adventures

Guided hiking trips in the wilderness around Lake Labarge and canoe trips. Dog-sled expeditions in winter. *Box 5076, Whitehorse, Canada, YT Y1A 4S3, Fax 867/668 26 33*

Edgewater

Nice little modern hotel at the centre of town. *30 rooms, 101 Main St., Tel. 867/667 25 72, Fax 668 30 14, Category 1–2*

Town & Mountain

A modern hotel at the centre of town. In-house restaurant and bar are convenient and well run. *30 rooms, 401 Main St., Tel. 867/668 76 44, Fax 668 58 22, Category 1–2*

You can enjoy good live country music in the *Roadhouse Saloon (2163 2nd Ave.)* or in the ❂ *Tavern* at the Kopper-King filling station *(mile 918.3, Alaska Hwy.)*.

Tourism Yukon

A big Visitor Centre on the Alaska Hwy. next to the Transportation Museum. *Postal address: P.O. Box 2703, Whitehorse, Canada, YT Y1A 2C6, Tel. 867/667 53 40, Fax 667 35 46, www.touryukon.com*

Faithful companions

They're always with you. Their buzzing lulls you off to sleep in your tent or camper. Blood-thirsty mosquitoes are ready and waiting to pounce on you out there in the woods, on lake shores and near marshes. What can you do about these ubiquitous pests? Loose-fitting clothes help. So do thick lumberjack shirts and relaxed-fit jeans. If your trousers are too tight-fitting, the bugs will bite right through them. If you're sleeping out in the wilds, you'll need mosquito nets at night. During the day you'll want to cover up your head and face in one. Rub any bare skin at all, even your ankles if you're wearing thin socks, with commercial repellents like Off or Cutter. Musk-ox oil is another possibility, as is (take it from an old hand) lamp kerosine.

Trappers' and gold prospectors' trails

These routes are marked in green on the map on the inside front cover and in the Road Atlas beginning on page 100

① THE KENAI PENINSULA: GLACIERS AND FJORDS

Green valleys, glacier-clad mountains and rocky inlets, where seals and sea otters bask in the sun and play in blue waters – the Kenai Peninsula is the perfect place for putting out your first feelers from Anchorage. If you're planning to stay a while in Alaska, this is the journey you should take, to find out how grand the wild North can be. You can do the 850-km trip, with time to spare, in five to six days. The best season for it is, thanks to the mild climate of this region, from mid-May to September.

You start off from the city of *Anchorage (p. 29)*, at the east end of the centre of town, where the *Seward Highway (Hwy. 1)* begins. Shopping malls and sprawling suburbs line the road but, after a half-hour drive, nature takes over with stunning views across fjords, mountains and tidal flats. The scenic ✴ highway follows the north coast of a long inlet, *Turnagain Arm (p. 35)*. Keep your eyes open: you might spot mountain sheep and bears on the rocks above the road. And salmon swim up the raging torrents to spawn in summer – a string of

cars parked along the road will tell you where people are watching. A tip: stock up on typical Alaskan provisions that will keep, such as smoked salmon, beef jerky and reindeer sausage, for your roadside picnics at *Indian Valley Meats* on Indian Road about 40 km from Anchorage.

If the weather's good you'd probably enjoy detouring to *Alyeska Resort (p. 34)*, where you can visit the historic *Crow Creek Mine* and take a gondola up for a scenic panorama of ✴ *the peak of Mt. Alyeska* up in the clouds. Not long after that, at the eastern end of Turnagain Arm, you'll reach *Portage Glacier (p. 35)*. Meltwater from it feeds a turquoise glacier lake in the mountains, which is dotted with ice calved from the glacier.

And on southwards: Highway 1 now curves along a raging white-water torrent, *Granite Creek*, before gradually climbing up into the Kenai Mountains. Particularly lovely: the broad valley with *Summit Lake*, where moose and elk graze in flowering meadows. Soon afterwards you can turn left at *Tern Lake Junction (observation platform for bird-watching)* and head south on Highway 9.

About 10 km down the road you can learn all about salmon. At the *Trail Lake Salmon Hatchery* illustrated panels are informative on the life cyle of the salmon. You can look at myriad fingerlings hatched in large ponds. In the small creek across from them, fiery red mature *sockeye salmon* spawn from mid-July until well into August. From here it's only about an hour's drive to the port of *Seward (p. 42)*. Your best bet is to stay here for at least two nights so you'll have plenty of time to enjoy a relaxing but exciting canoe or kayak trip in *Kenai Fjords National Park (p. 43)*, or a beautiful hike to *Exit Glacier* or even a scenic flight over the glaciers.

From Seward your route takes you back to Tern Lake Junction and from there westward to Highway 1 (here it's called Sterling Highway). A spate of lovely little lakes will invite you to picnic or linger and camp at superb camping sites. The road keeps coming back to the magnificent *Kenai River*, teeming with salmon. On its banks, at *Cooper Landing* and the town of *Sterling*, you can watch fishers in waders (hip-length dull green rubber boots) or buy a fishing licence for a few dollars and cast some flies (spinners) into the river yourself.

After stocking up on supplies at *Soldotna (p. 40)*, turn off on to a side-road and head for *Kenai*, which was founded by the Russians. Cut straight across the Kenai River delta and continue south on *Kalifornski Beach Road* with breathtaking views across Cook Inlet to the snow-mantled volcanoes across the bay.

At *Kasilof* the road again joins Sterling Highway, which now follows the steep coastline of the Kenai Peninsula on south. Here too you'll have superb views out across the sea. The dark sand and pebble beaches at the foot of the cliffs are marvellous for long walks. At *Clam Gulch* you can dig for delicious Razor Clams (don't cut your feet: their shells are razor-sharp!). Not far away is a Russian Orthodox church perched on a hill above the sea at the Native American settlement of *Ninilchik.*

Sterling Highway rises once again into green hills and then you go downhill for quite a way until you come upon *Homer (p. 38)* at the bottom, where the highway ends. This is another place where you should spend two nights to have a whole day for a *boat trip* on which you can watch birds, otters and seals. Alternatively, you might want to visit the isolated fishing village of *Seldovia (p. 40)*. You will find that it is possible to drive the 400 km back to Anchorage in a day.

② THE PANHANDLE: ALASKA BY SEA

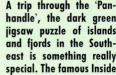

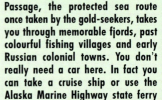

A trip through the 'Panhandle', the dark green jigsaw puzzle of islands and fjords in the Southeast is something really special. The famous Inside Passage, the protected sea route once taken by the gold-seekers, takes you through memorable fjords, past colourful fishing villages and early Russian colonial towns. You don't really need a car here. In fact you can take a cruise ship or use the Alaska Marine Highway state ferry line and enjoy the region to the fullest. Going by ferry takes two to three days, but you should really plan to make some stops along the way and stay for one to two days at each place you stop.

Cruise ships usually leave for Alaska from Vancouver. The big car ferries, on the other hand, depart from Bellingham near Seattle as well as Prince Rupert in Canada. No matter where you set out from, your first Alaskan port of call is *Ketchikan (p. 63)*, which is the beginning of Tlingit Indian country. Be sure to look out for the big *totem pole parks, Saxman* and *Totem Bight (p. 64)*, on the outskirts of Ketchikan.

The next place the ferry stops is *Wrangell (p. 71)*, which is a very good place to stop if you are travelling on your own and not in a group. It's a rather rough and tumble fishing village, but you can make the acquaintance of the locals here. Moreover, you can leave from Wrangell to go on trips by boat and bush plane to the *mouth of the Stikine River,* to *LeConte Glacier* and to watch burly *brown bears salmon fishing on Anan Creek (p. 71)*.

North of Wrangell begin the ◁▷ *Wrangell Narrows,* a particularly beautiful part of the Inside Passage. Along the waterway between Kupreanof and Mitkof Island, which is often only 100 m across, American bald eagles nest in towering Douglas firs, seals bask in the sun on rocks and whales sometimes come close to the ship. Via *Petersburg (p. 66)* the Inland Passage route goes through wide *Frederick Sound* (an excellent place for whale-watching!) and on to *Sitka (p. 67)*, which is on the western shore of Baranof Island – an interesting port of call

for history buffs. Here they can find traces of the 18th- and 19th-century Russian colonial era. (Remember, not all state ferries take the Sitka route! Check before you book if you want to stop there.)

Your next port of call: the port of Auke Bay near *Juneau (p. 61)*, Alaska's capital. You should plan on staying a few days here too as the city is the point of departure for tours into the icy realm of *Glacier Bay (p. 58)* and for excursions by air, canoe and kayak to the glacier-encircled fjord called *Tracy Arm.*

The last lap of your northbound cruise up the Inland Passage is on the 150-km-long *Lynn Canal*: the mountains close in on the ever narrowing fjord. The waterfalls rushing down the green slopes are higher here. More glaciers come into view. At the northern end of the fjord you have two choices. If you're travelling by car and want to go on into the interior, you can drive off the ferry at *Haines (p. 60)* and drive out on to Haines Highway. However, it's much more scenic and exciting to follow in the footsteps of the gold prospectors and continue on up the Inside Passage to *Skagway (p. 68)*. From there you can drive on into the Canadian Yukon and the Klondike.

③ IN THE GOLD PROSPECTORS' FOOTSTEPS: FROM SKAGWAY TO DAWSON CITY

Roughly 30,000 hardy adventurers left Skagway in the winter of 1898 and crossed the mountains to go north up the Yukon River to the gold-fields in the Klondike. A historic trek, one that history buffs can retrace on the old trails or comfortably in their cars on modern highways. The wilderness has remained unchanged since those days. It takes about three to four days to drive the 500 km to the Klondike. If you're going by canoe, you'd better allow yourself at least two weeks.

Like the pioneers, start from *Skagway (p. 68)*, which is easily accessible by state ferry or by air from the south. Even in the Gold Rush era this was the last place to stock up on provisions before the trackless interior. On the modern *Klondike Highway 2* it takes only about four hours of steep uphill driving via ❦ *White Pass* at an elevation of 1,003 m and the pioneer settlement of *Carcross* through a chain of lakes to get to the upper reaches of the Yukon River and Whitehorse.

The old route across *Chilkoot Pass (p. 70)*, at an elevation of 1,067 m, still exists in the form of a good wilderness trail (from July). It ends at Lake Bennet, where a shuttle bus service picks up hikers and takes them to Whitehorse. It takes about four to five days to reach and cross the pass – imagine the hardships the pioneers had to endure. The gold-seekers had to haul tonnes of baggage over the pass with provisions and equipment to last an entire year. At the top of the Pass, Mounties of the Royal Canadian Mounted Police used to check whether every prospector had brought with him what he needed. Prospectors had to go up and down the steep ridge of the Coast Mountains 30 to 40 times to bring up their equipment. In the dead of winter, too! Today's backpackers

perspiring under the weight of 20 kg in summer should be inspired by those heroic exploits.

After a day of rest in *Whitehorse (p. 84)*, where you can visit the old paddle-wheel steamer *SS Klondike* and *Miles Canyon* to imbibe even more history on site, your journey north continues. The route now follows the Yukon River, which widens out from here on. The Klondike Highway is paved and it takes two days of easy driving through silent forests and uninhabited valleys to reach the Gold Rush town of *Dawson City (p. 80)*. For rest and photo breaks we recommend *Lake Labarge, Five Finger Rapids* and *Moose Creek Lodge*, which has a fantastically good bakery to stave travellers' hunger pangs.

A much more historically authentic and certainly exciting route is the one taken by the gold prospectors in the late 19th and early 20th centuries. By canoe it takes from six to seven days to reach Dawson City *(canoe and equipment rental in Whitehorse)*. If you opt for this route, drift lazily down the broad Yukon River, watching moose and bears along the banks, casting an idle line overboard (the fish don't bite all that often) and enjoying the peacefulness of nature. Civilization starts again at the confluence of the Yukon and the Klondike rivers, where you will reach *Dawson City (p. 80)*. After hiking and canoeing all the way from Skagway, you'll find Dawson City looks like a metropolis. You can empathize with the weary prospectors who viewed the gold-fields as the Promised Land at the end of the trail.

Practical information

Important addresses and useful information for your visit to Alaska

ALCOHOL

In Alaska the purchase of alcoholic drinks is permitted only in bars, liquor stores and package stores. Alcohol may not be purchased by or served to anyone under the age of 21. In the Canadian Yukon Territory, 19-year-olds will be served alcohol in saloons. Inuit and Native American settlements in the Yukon are 'dry'. No alcohol is served there and you may not bring any in.

AMERICAN & BRITISH ENGLISH

Marco Polo travel guides are written in British English. In North America, certain terms and usages deviate from British usage. Some of the more frequently encountered examples are:
baggage for luggage, billion for milliard, cab for taxi, car rental for car hire, drugstore for chemist's, fall for autumn, first floor for ground floor, freeway/highway for motorway, gas(oline) for petrol, railroad for railway, restroom for toilet/lavatory, streetcar for tram, subway for underground/tube, toll-free numbers for freephone numbers, trailer for caravan, trunk for boot, vacation for holiday, wait staff for waiting staff

(in restaurants etc.), zip code for postal code.

CAMPING

Public camping sites are the most scenic, usually on lakes and in national or State parks. They have fire pits, wooden picinic tables, water pumps and outdoor toilets. Spending the night at one of these costs $5–$10. There are also private camp sites with hot showers, small shops and sometimes even swimming pools, on the outskirts of towns and outside the parks (prices: $10–$30). You can also camp anywhere else you want except in the parks. However, pitching tents near towns is frowned on.

Watch out for bears! This is no joke. At night stow food in your car so they can't smell it. If you're camping in the woods and don't have a car, hang food at least four metres off the ground in a tree, far from your tent.

CAR RENTAL

You must be 25 to rent a car (from 21 for a surcharge) and you must have a credit card. Your country's driving licence is valid.

Book cars or caravans several months in advance through your travel agent. That's usually cheaper and less of a hassle than trying to find something when you get there since caravans especially are booked up in peak season. It is much cheaper to return your vehicle to the place where you picked it up.

CLIMATE & WHEN TO GO

Most of Alaska and the Yukon have a northern continental climate with surprisingly warm, dry summers and good weather lasting for weeks on end (in Fairbanks July temperatures can be over 30°C [86°F]), but winters are bitterly cold. In South Alaska and the Panhandle the sea makes the climate milder. Clouds over the Pacific ensure abundant precipitation: a lot of rain in summer and snow in winter.

The best time for travelling to Alaska and the Yukon is from mid-July to late August. However, September can be just as lovely, with sunny, clear days and cool nights. Early in September, colder weather turns the leaves of birch and aspen gold and the tundra in the north glows red and yellow for a week or two. The peak tourist season is July and August, when all American and Canadian children have their long summer holiday. Hotels in the cities and national parks are booked up then. If you do want to (or can only) travel then, be sure to make reservations as far in advance as you possibly can. The peak season for dog-sledding and skiing is, of course, mid-February to mid-April.

CONSULATES

Canada and Great Britain have no consular offices in Alaska. The nearest consulates are in Seattle, Washington.

in the United States:
British Consulate
900 Fourth Avenue, Suite 3001, Seattle, WA 98164,
Tel. 206/622 92 55, Fax 622 47 28
Canadian Consulate General
412 Plaza 600 – 6th & Stewart Street, Seattle, WA 98101-1286,
Tel. 206/443 17 77, Fax 443 96 62

in Canada:
United States Consulate
1059 West Pender Street, Vancouver, British Columbia, Canada V6E 2M6, Tel. 604/685 43 11
British Consulate
1111 Melville St., Suite 800, Vancouver British Columbia, Canada, V6E 3V6, Tel. 604/683 44 21

CURRENCY

In the Yukon Territory the currency is the Canadian dollar (Can $). *Banks* are usually open from 10 am to 3 pm. They cash travellers' cheques (made out in US dollars), usually at a good exchange rate, but do not change European, Asian or African currency.

You should take several different kinds of legal tender with you: several hundred dollars in *cash*, as well as *travellers' cheques* in US dollars (they are accepted everywhere in shops and restaurants and you are given change) as well as a *credit card* (Visa or Mastercard) for expenses like car hire and emergencies. Credit cards are accepted everywhere in hotels, restaurants, shops and filling stations. ATMs (cashpoints) accept *US* and *Canadian* cards.

CUSTOMS

Plants, meat, fruit and other agricultural products may not be brought into Alaska and Canada. Adults may bring in 200 cigarettes or 50 cigars or 2 kg tobacco as well as 1.1 l of spirits. Also presents worth up to $100.

You may bring back to Great Britain: 1 l spirits over 22%, 200 cigarettes or 100 cigarillos or 50 cigars or 250 g tobacco, 50 g perfume or 250 g eau de toilette and other articles for personal use.

DOMESTIC FLIGHTS

Flying is part of everyday life in Alaska because many settlements and lodges in the interior can be reached only by air. Alaska Airlines serves all large towns and cities. In small towns and settlements you can use any of the reliable local companies, such as Reeve Aleutian Airways, Pen-Air and ERA-Air in Anchorage, Frontier Flying Service in Fairbanks, LAB Flying Service or Glacier-Air in Juneau. Visitors from abroad are offered discounts by Alaska Airlines and several regional services.

Remember to book all the tickets you'll need from home before you reach Alaska. However, you can book an air taxi in Alaska or Canada. Air taxis will take you anywhere you want to go in the wilderness. Alaskan bush pilots will set you down on any lake or sandbank, at charter prices ranging from $200 to $300 an hour in the air. The further you fly north, the more expensive it is. Don't forget to book a return ticket.

DRIVING

UK nationals: in the United States you must be 21 to rent a car; rates may be higher for those under 25. Your national driving licence is valid on trips of up to three months (in the Canadian Yukon Territory only one month!). Seat belts must be fastened. In Alaska and the Yukon you must drive with your headlights on during the day.

All major Alaska highways are paved but some of them are in very bad condition since frost heaves make the tarmac buckle every spring. The speed limit on country roads is usually 55 mph (88 km/h), in towns 35 mph (50 km/h). Traffic regulations are similar to European ones with the following exceptions: at traffic lights you may turn right even when the light is red. Overtaking on the right is tolerated on highways with several lanes. You may not overtake schoolbuses if the blinking light signal is on and oncoming traffic must also stop. There is also something called *three-way-* or *four-way stops*, intersections at which vehicles coming from all directions must stop. The first to stop is also the first to drive on.

EMERGENCIES

In cities the emergency number to call is '911', toll-free from all telephones. In rural areas other numbers may be given on callbox phones for police, fire and doctors on emergency duty. When in doubt, dial *operator* ('0').

FERRIES

The big, comfortable car ferries operated by the Alaska Marine

Highway run between all large Southeast Alaska ports along the famous Inside Passage as well as Valdez, Cordova, Whittier, Seward, Homer and Kodiak Island in southern Alaska. Once a month a ferry also goes from Homer along the Aleutian Islands as far as Dutch Harbor. If you are travelling with a car or caravan or want a cabin, you should make reservations four or five months in advance (Alaska Marine Highway, Information, Box 25535, Juneau 99802-5535, Tel. 907/465 39 41 or 1-800 642 00 66, Fax 907/277 48 29. On the Internet: *www.dot.state.ak.us/external/amhs/home.html*). Foot passengers with or without bicycles do not usually need to book in advance.

HEALTH

Health care is excellent but expensive. In an emergency you may be flown out by park rangers or air ambulance to the nearest hospital. You must buy a valid health insurance policy before leaving home. If you're going on a wilderness trip, take a good first-aid kit with you. If you really do have to drink water from mountain streams (never from rivers!), boil it for at least 7 minutes before drinking it.

HUNTING & FISHING

If you want to hunt in Alaska or in the Canadian Yukon Territory, you are required by law to have a local guide and a hunting licence issued for specified species of game. Find out about this from Visitors' Centres. Fishing, on the other hand, is open to everyone in all lakes and rivers. All you need is a visitor's fishing licence, which you can buy in sporting-goods stores and lodges. You'll receive a brochure explaining the regulations and *bag limits.* You need a special fishing licence to fish for king salmon or to fish anywhere in national parks. If what you're after is a fishing holiday, you should book rooms in a fishing lodge in the back country, where experienced local guides will show you the best spots for good catches. Price: $2,000–$6,000 a week. Fishing boats can be chartered for halibut and salmon fishing in Homer, Seward, Valdez and many other coastal towns.

INFORMATION

in the United States:
Alaska State Division of Tourism
P.O. Box 110801,
Juneau, AK 99811, USA,
Tel. 907/465 20 12, Fax 465 37 67
e-mail: gonorth@commerce.state.ak.us;
www.dced.state.ak.us/tourism/homenew.htm

in the Yukon:
Tourism Yukon
P.O. Box 2703 Whitehorse,
Yukon Territory Y1A 2C6,
Tel. 867/667 53 40,
Fax 867/667 35 46;
e-mail: info@touryukon.com.;
Internet: www.touryukon.com

in Great Britain:
Alaska Tourist Information Board
c/o Bywater Communications 2,
The Billings, Walnut Tree Close,
Guildford, Surrey, GU1 4YD
Tel. 014 83 45 71 77,
Fax 014 83 45 13 61

Visit Canada Centre
62-65 Trafalgar Square,
London WC2 5DY,
Tel. 08 91 71 50 00

In Alaska you'll find Information Centres and Visitors' Bureaux – they are very clearly signposted – in every town and city, national park and even the smallest settlements. In Anchorage, Tok, Fairbanks and Ketchikan there are also outstanding Public Lands Information Centres (PLICs), where you'll get material and maps on national parks and other nature reserves. You can also book cabins and space at camping sites at PLICs.

OPENING HOURS

Most shops are open Mon to Sat from 9.30 am to 6 pm. Urban shopping malls stay open from 10 am to 9 pm and Sun from 12 to 5 pm. Supermarkets and general stores in small towns are often open until late at night and at weekends. In spring and autumn museums and other tourist attractions often have shorter opening hours than in peak season. In winter they often close down altogether.

PASSPORT & VISA

To enter Alaska Canadians need only an ID card. For a longer stay, carry a passport. UK subjects also need only passports. On entry, whether by air or overland, you must fill out a landing card for the immigration authorities. To enter the Yukon in Canada, US citizens and permanent US residents do not need passports or other documents. You should carry identification (green card or birth certificate). US citizens who enter Canada from third countries need valid passports or naturalization certificates. Permanent US residents need green cards. British subjects need only a valid passport for a stay of up to six months.

You may have to show a return ticket on arrival and proof of adequate finances. Visas, which must be obtained in advance from the nearest US consulate, are only necessary if you plan to stay longer than three months. Customs and immigration formalities will be taken care of at the first US airport you land. Your flight from there to Alaska is a domestic one.

POST

Post offices are open Mon to Fri 9 am to 6 pm and Sat 8 am to noon. Airmail letters to the European Union: 60 c, postcards 50 c (in Canada 90 c). A card takes about seven days to reach Europe from cities. From the back country it'll take three to four days longer.

PUBLIC TRANSPORT

Several regional private bus companies, such as Alaskon Express, Alaska Direct Bus Lines and Norline Coaches, link all towns along the Alaska highways and in the Canadian Yukon Territory. Of course they don't run every hour. You might even have to wait a day or two for the next bus. Another problem with bus travel is that it's often quite a long way from bus terminals to any attractions you want to visit or trailheads where your hike starts.

A really scenic way to see a beautiful section of Alaska in comfort is by taking the Alaska Railroad from Anchorage through Denali National Park to Fairbanks (the trip takes 12 hours). The trip from Anchorage to Seward takes about four hours. A train shuttles between Portage and Whittier with connections to the ferries in Prince William Sound. Find out from your travel agent or, when you get to Alaska, call Tel. *907/265 24 94.*

TAXES

There is no official sales tax in Alaska yet cities and districts are permitted to levy up to 6% *sales tax* surcharge. In Canada there is a VAT tax, called GST, of 7%. All taxes are added on bills so they are not included in the prices listed on menus and merchandise.

TELEPHONE

All telephone numbers in Alaska and in the Canadian Yukon Territory have seven digits. Long-distance calls have a three-digit *area code (dialling code).* The state of Alaska has 907 as its area code; the Yukon Territory has area code 867.

Local calls from call-boxes cost 25–30 c; a computerized voice tells you the rates for long distance calls after you have dialled. Dial the telephone number only for local calls. For long-distance calls within the state dial '1' before the number. Be careful in hotels. They often demand high surcharges for calls!

It's cheaper to telephone if you use an American telephone credit card (such as an AT & T one), which you can obtain at no extra charge from most credit-card firms in Britain and Europe.

If you encounter problems with placing calls, the *operator* ('0') will help you. The operator also places *collect calls.* Toll-free numbers, such as those of car-hire firms or hotels, are preceded by 1-800.

The dialling code for Great Britain is: 011 44, followed by the local area code (dialling code) without the first zero and then the number. The dialling code from Britain to Alaska and Canada is 001.

TIME ZONES

The difference in time between Great Britain and Alaska is 9 h; the two westernmost Aleutian Islands: 10 h; the Yukon Territory 8 h. Daylight savings time in Alaska and Canada: first Sunday in April, add one hour – last Sunday in October, set clocks back one hour.

TIPPING

A service charge is not included in menu prices. Therefore you should leave about 15% of the bill as a *tip* on your table when you leave. Bell-boys in hotels or at lodges receive a tip of about $1 per piece of luggage. You give your trail or fishing guide a tip of $5–$10 a day.

VOLTAGE

110 volt, 60 hertz. You'll have to bring a plug adapter for your (adaptable!) hair dryer or electric shaver.

WEIGHTS & MEASURES

The Canadian Yukon Territory is on the metric system. However, in Alaska, like everywhere else in the US, you eat up the miles (= 1.6 km) on the highways, buy petrol (gasoline) in gallons (= 3.7 l) and freeze your socks off on the glaciers in degrees Fahrenheit: (0°C = 32°F, 15°C = 59°F, 20°C = 68°F, 25°C = 77°F).

The most important conversions:

1 cm	0.39 inches
1 m	1.09 yd (3.28 ft)
1 km	0.62 miles
1 m²	1.20 sq. yards
1 ha	2.47 acres
1 km²	0.39 sq. miles
1 g	0.035 ounces
1 kg	2.21 pounds
1 British tonne	1016 kg
1 US ton	907 kg

1 litre is equivalent to 0.22 Imperial gallons and 0.26 US gallons

YOUTH HOSTELS

The ten Alaskan hostels belonging to the American Youth Hostel organization, Hostelling International, are listed in a book available at booksellers: *Hostelling International Handbook, Vol. 2.*

In many places there are also simple backpacker hostelries with bunks costing $10–$20 a night. You'd better bring your own sleeping bag.

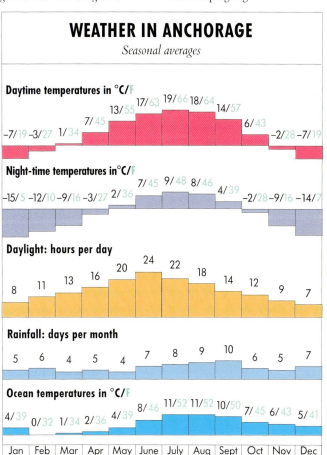

WEATHER IN ANCHORAGE
Seasonal averages

Daytime temperatures in °C/F

–7/19 –3/27 1/34 7/45 13/55 17/63 19/66 18/64 14/57 6/43 –2/28 –7/19

Night-time temperatures in°C/F

–15/5 –12/10 –9/16 –3/27 2/36 7/45 9/48 8/46 4/39 –2/28 –9/16 –14/7

Daylight: hours per day

8 11 13 16 20 24 22 18 14 12 9 7

Rainfall: days per month

5 6 4 5 4 7 8 9 10 6 5 7

Ocean temperatures in °C/F

4/39 0/32 1/34 2/36 4/39 8/46 11/52 11/52 10/50 7/45 6/43 5/41

Jan	Feb	Mar	Apr	May	June	July	Aug	Sept	Oct	Nov	Dec

Do's and don'ts

*The Alaskan wilderness can be dangerous and there are
some points you should be informed about*

If you're careful, Alaska is quite a safe place to travel in. However, there are a few points to remember. In one respect Alaska isn't all that different from most places. Don't leave cameras in your car where thieves can see them and do lock your motel-room door.

Bear spray
The pepper spray sold at Alaskan sporting-goods stores may deter bears, but never take a can of it with you in charter planes. Airlines forbid this anyway because the spray could go off accidentally and temporarily blind the pilot. Needless to say, a serious accident could result!

Don't underestimate distances
Don't kid yourself about how big Alaska is. The north especially is vast indeed. What is only a finger's breadth on the map can easily mean a day's hard drive over bumpy unpaved roads.

Be tactful
Alaska has always been macho country. Late in the evening things can get pretty rough and wild in saloons and bars so it's always better not to contradict people or start arguments. You don't want to get into a fight with a lumberjack or a fisherman loaded to the gills. You or your partner might wake up in hospital.

Be careful about road conditions
You can't rely on highways being in good condition throughout. Even if you're on a section of road that has been recently surfaced so you think you can get away with driving 60 mph, you'll probably find out that frost heaves are waiting for you a mile down the road to bump you back to the reality of driving in Alaska.

Wilderness hiking
Whether you're planning to spend a day, a week or a month hiking or canoeing through the wilderness, remember to leave an exact description of the route you'll be taking and the date by which you expect to be back with the canoe-rental firm, the bush pilot who is flying you into the back country or a national park ranger. If anything should go wrong, help can be sent to you. (Don't forget to report back to any of the above as soon as you've returned safely!) Take provisions with you for several extra days just in case you need them!

Road Atlas of Alaska and the Yukon

*Please refer to back cover for an overview
of this Road Atlas*

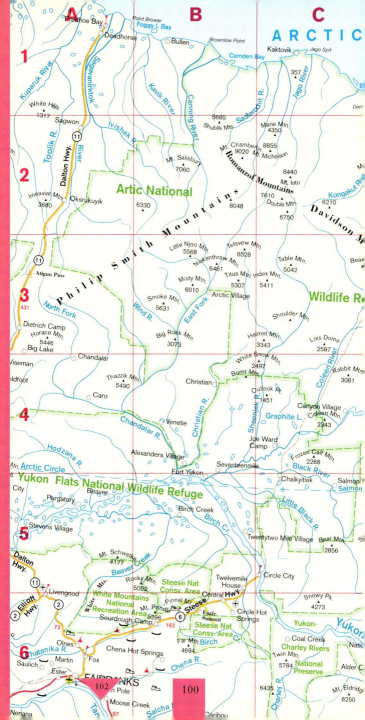

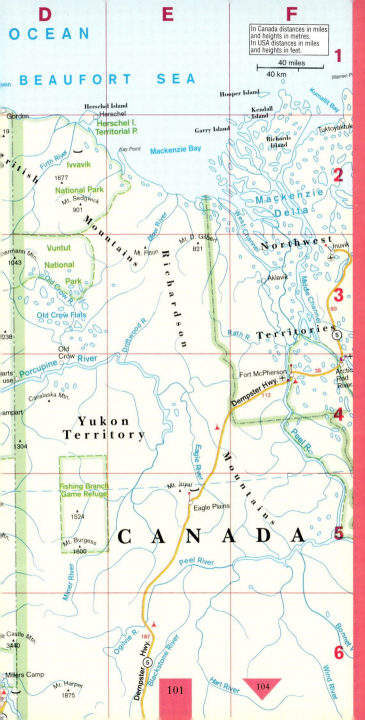

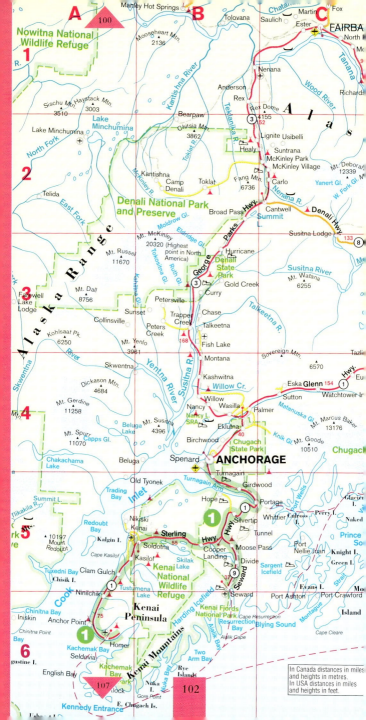

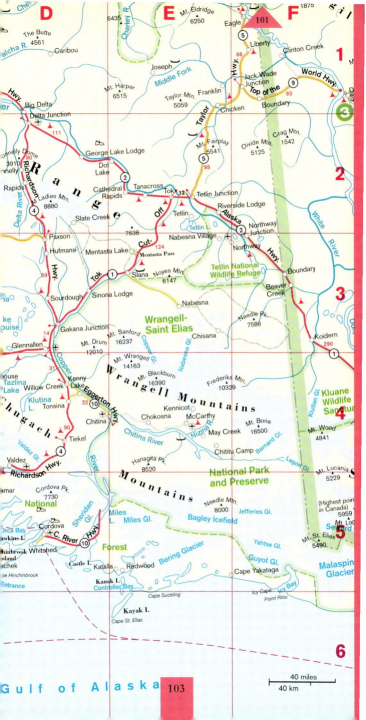

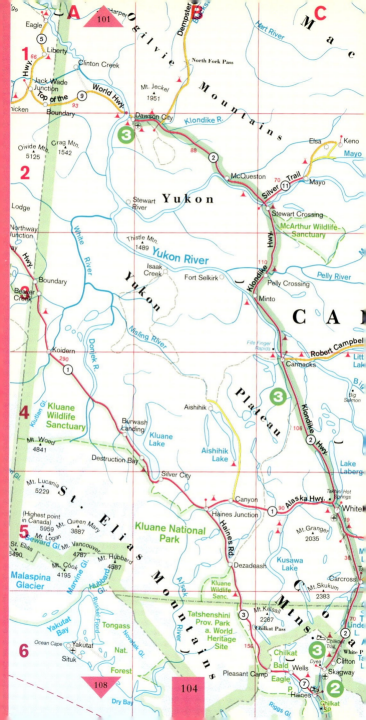

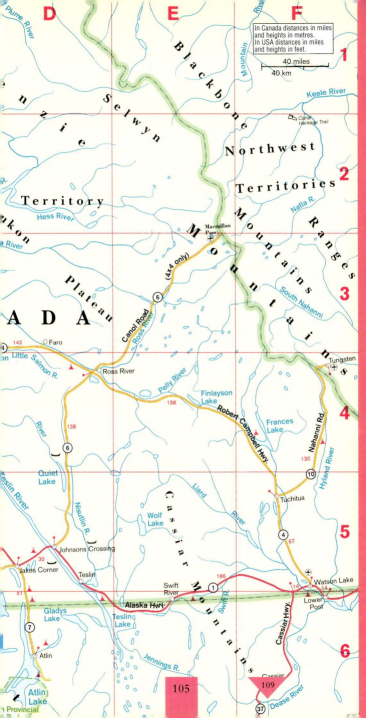

A   **B**   **C**

Kegun Lake   Kagati Lake   Eek Lake   Togio   9982   Shotgun Hills 3388

Kwethluk River   **K i l b u c k**

Nefornak   Tuntutuliak   Akulurak

1   Kipnuk   Kulvagavik   Eek   **M o u n t a i n s**

Kwigillingok   Kanektok   River   Nuyakuk Lake   Chikuminuk Lake   Nuyaku

Kuskokwim Bay   Quinhagak   **Togiak National**   **Wood-Tikchik State Park**

Jacksmith Bay   Togiak Lake   Lake Beverley

Alkun Mountains   Lake Nerka

Carter Spit   Goodnews Bay   **Wildlife**   Kashiagamiut   Lake Aleknagik

2   Goodnews Bay   **Refuge**   Togiak   Aleknagik

Platinum   Ungalikthluk   Sparks   Dillingham   Kanakanak

Chagvan Bay   **Togiak Bay**   Ekuk

Tongue Point   Rocky Point   Nushagak Bay

Cape Newenham   Hagemeister Island   Crooked I.   Etolin Point

Cape Peirce   Calm Point   **Walrus Is.**   Round I.   **Nushagak Peninsula**

Walrus I. State Game Sanctuary   Protection Point   **Kviche**

Cape Constantine

3   **Egegik Ba**   Goose Point

        B r i s t o l   B a y

B E R I N G   S E A   Ugashik Bay

4   Port Heiden   Meshik   Aniakchak Vulkan   **Aniakcha Natio Monu and Preser**

Strogonof Point   Port Heiden

Ilnik   Black Peak   Kujulik Bay

3385   Cape Kum

P   Chignik Bay   Nakcha

Chignik Lake   Chignik   Castle Cape

Bear River   Sandy L.   Mt. Veniaminof

5   Port Moller   **a**   7075   **Alaska Peninsula National Wildlife Refuge**   Perryville

Cape Rozinof   **Port Moller**   **k**   Seal Cape

Herendeen Bay   **s**   Kupreanof Peninsula   Mitrofania I.

Caribou R.   **l**   **a**   Jacob I.

A   Stepovak Bay   Bluff Point

Izembek National Wildlife Refuge and Wilderness   Pavlof   Kupreanof Point

offet Point   Pavlof Bay   Unga Strait   Korovin I.

nbek   Beaver Bay   Sand Point

oon   Long John   Unga I.   Popof I.

d Bay   King Cove   Ukolnoi I.   Squaw Harbor   Big Koninji Island

6   Dolgoi Island   West Nagai Strait   Little Koninji Island

Deer Island   Nagai I.   East Nagai Strait   Simeonof Island

Unalaska Island   **Shumag**   Otter Strait

Sanak Island   Pauloff Harbor   Caton I.

106

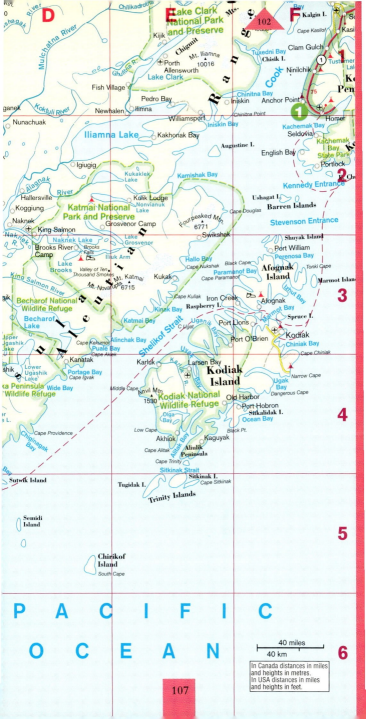

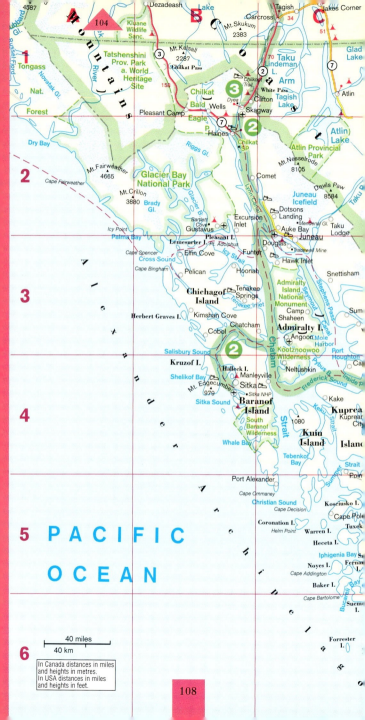

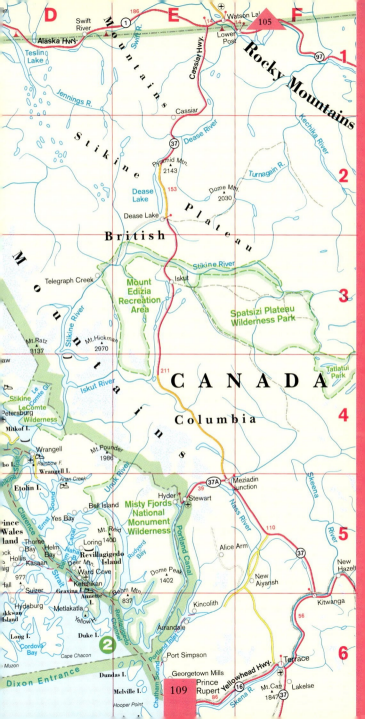

ROAD ATLAS LEGEND

——————	Befestigter Highway Surfaced highway		Verkehrsflughafen Airport
——————	Unbefestigter Highway Unmaid highway	⊕	Flugplatz Airfield
——————	Hauptstraße Main road	+	Landeplatz Airstrip
············	Nebenstraße Minor road	▲ 6255	Höhenangaben in Fuß Heights in feet
- - - - - -	Piste Track	12	Entfernungen in Meilen Distances in miles
③	Straßennummer Road number	⊖	Grenzübergang Check-point
——————	Eisenbahn Railway	▲	Camping Holiday camp
– – – – –	Schiffsverbindung Shipping line	🥾	Wandern Trekking
– – – – –	Polarkreis Arctic circle	⌣	Kanu Canoe
▨▨▨	Staatsgrenze National boundary	⋊	Paß Pass
▨▨▨	Provinzgrenze Provincial boundary	·	Objekt Object
⌐ – – ¬	Nationalpark, Naturpark, Naturschutzgebiet National park, nature park, nature reserve		
░░░	Gletscher Glacier		
∼∼∼	Fluß River		

In Canada heights in metres !

|—— 40 miles ——|
|—— 40 km ——|

110

This index lists all major place-names and attractions to visit, including museums and National Parks (NP). Numerals in italics refer to photographs and those in bold face to main entries.

Place-names

Anchorage 7, 19, 23, 26, 27, *28*, **29**, 95
Atlin, B.C. 80
Barrow 20, **74**
Copper Center 38
Cordova 26, 27, **45**, 94
Dawson City 10, 23, 27, **80**, *81*
Delta Junction 50
Dutch Harbor/ Unalaska **74**, 94
Eagle 9, 27, **52**
Fairbanks 6, 8, 10, 14, 15, 23, 26, 27, **52**, *54*, 95
Glennallen 38
Gustavus/ Glacier Bay NP 58
Haines 17, 27, 57, **60**
Homer 26, **38**, 94
Hope 40
Hyder 27, 57, **65**
Juneau *12*, 15, 16, 27, *56*, **61**
Kenai/Soldotna 27, **40**
Ketchikan 17, 26, **63**, 95
Kodiak 27
Kotzebue 76
McCarthy 46
Nenana 26, **55**
Nome 6, 10, 11, 15, 20, *21*, 26, 27, **77**
Palmer 27, **42**
Petersburg 27, **66**
Seldovia 40
Seward 6, 26, 27, **42**, 94
Sitka 11, 17, **67**
Skagway 10, 27, 57, **68**, *70*
Soldotna/Kenai 40
Talkeetna *8*, 9, 27, **55**
Tok **55**, 95
Unalaska/ Dutch Harbor **74**, 94
Valdez 9, 11, 16, 26, 27, **44**, 94
Watson Lake 84
Whitehorse 26, **84**, *85*
Whittier 27, **46**, 94
Wrangell 71

Attractions to visit

Admiralty Island/ Pack Creek 62
Alaska Aviation Heritage Museum, Anchorage 31
Alaskaland, Fairbanks 53
Alaska Raptor Rehabilitation Center, Sitka 67

Alaska SeaLife Center 43
Alaska State Museum, Juneau 62
Aleutian Islands **74**, 94
Alyeska Resort/ Girdwood 34
Anan Creek 71
Anchorage Museum of History and Art 31
Bar of the Alaskan Hotel, Juneau 61
Big Delta State Historical Park 50
Board of Trade Saloon, Nome 77
Bonanza Creek 82
Chilkoot Trail 70
Chugach State Park 35
Dalton Highway 54
Dawson City Museum, Dawson City 81
Dempster Highway 82
Denali NP *4*, **8**, *48*, **50**, *52*
Denali Park Road 51
Eklutna Village *34*, 35
Fort Abercrombie State Park 76
Fort William H. Seward, Haines 60
Gastineau Salmon Hatchery, Juneau 61
Gates of the Arctic NP 75
Glacier Bay Country Inn, Gustavus 59
Glacier Bay NP 58, *59*
Gold Dredge No. 8, Fairbanks 53
Haines Junction/ Kluane NP 83
Hatcher Pass Road 42
Hot Springs, Fairbanks 54
Iditarod Trail Committee, Palmer 42
K2 Aviation, Talkeetna 55
Katmai NP 9, 14, *72*, **75**
Kenai Fjords NP 7, *41*, **43**
Kennecott Mine *36*, 47
Klondike Gold Rush National Historical Park, Skagway 69
Kluane NP/ Haines Junction 10, **83**
Kobuk Valley NP 9, 73, 77
Kodiak bears, Kodiak Island 76
Kodiak Island 13, 26, 73, 74, **76**, 94
Lake Hood 31
Lake Louise 38

MacBride Museum, Whitehorse 85
McCarthy/Wrangell- St. Elias NP 46
Matanuska Glacier 42
Mendenhall Glacier 61
Misty Fjords National Monument 65
Nahanni NP 84
North Pole 55
Oomingmak Co-op, Anchorage 33
Pack Creek/Admiralty Island 13, **62**
Portage Glacier 35
Pratt Museum, Homer 39
Pribilof Islands 77
Prince William Sound 7, 16, *44*, **45**
Resolution Park, Anchorage 31
Richardson Highway 46
Riverboat Discovery, Fairbanks 53
Russian Bishop's House, Sitka 68
Salty Dawg Saloon, Homer 40
Santa Claus House, North Pole 55
Seward Highway 44
Sheldon Jackson Museum, Sitka 68
Sitka National Historical Park, Sitka 68
SS Klondike, Whitehorse 85
Top of the World Highway 82
Totem Bight Historical Park 64
Totem Heritage Center, Ketchikan 64
Totem poles, Ketchikan 64
Trail of '98 Museum, Skagway 69
Turnagain Arm 35
University Museum, Fairbanks 53
Valdez Museum 45
Valley of Ten Thousand Smokes, Katmai NP 75, 76
White Pass & Yukon Route 70
Wrangell-St. Elias NP/McCarthy 46, *47*
Yukon Transportation Museum 85

What do you get for your money?

The exchange rate with the dollar is volatile. Never-theless, even when it's high, trips to Alaska are still feasible, thanks to bargain prices in flights and package deals. Still you should remember that overhead costs are relatively high in Alaska since nearly all goods have to be imported from the south. The currency used in the Yukon Territory is the Canadian dollar (Can $), which tends to be about 25 per cent lower than the US $.

Let's compare the purchasing power of a few basic items. Breakfast costs about $5–$8; in better hotels and lodges you can expect to pay $10–$15. There is an extra charge for coffee of about $1.50–$2. You'll have to fork out about $3–$5 for a glass of beer in a bar. A bottle of imported lager costs at least $4. A thick, juicy prime steak can set you back $15–$20. Staying at a wilderness lodge costs $120–$350 a day. A fishing licence limited to two weeks costs $30 but a year's licence costs only $50. A gallon (3.7 l) of petrol (gasoline) costs anywhere from $1.20 to $2.50. A three-hour guided kayak trip comes to $ 50–$70. You'll lay out about $70–$110 including lunch for a day trip in a boat to watch animals or whales. You can rent a canoe for $25 a day and for $150 a week.

US $	UK £	Can $
1	0.62	1.49
2	1.25	2.98
3	1.87	4.47
4	2.49	5.96
5	3.12	7.45
10	6.23	14.91
20	12.46	29.82
30	18.69	44.72
40	24.93	59.63
50	31.16	74.54
60	37.39	89.45
70	43.62	104.36
80	49.85	119.26
90	56.08	134.17
100	62.31	149.08
200	124.63	298.16
300	185.90	446.76
400	247.87	595.68
500	311.57	745.40
750	467.35	1,118.10
1,000	623.13	1,490.80